Trade and Migration

Building Bridges for Global Labour Mobility

OECD

ORGANISATION FOR ECONOMIC CO-OPERATION AND DEVELOPMENT
THE WORLD BANK
INTERNATIONAL ORGANIZATION FOR MIGRATION

ORGANISATION FOR ECONOMIC CO-OPERATION AND DEVELOPMENT

Pursuant to Article 1 of the Convention signed in Paris on 14th December 1960, and which came into force on 30th September 1961, the Organisation for Economic Co-operation and Development (OECD) shall promote policies designed:

- to achieve the highest sustainable economic growth and employment and a rising standard of living in member countries, while maintaining financial stability, and thus to contribute to the development of the world economy;
- to contribute to sound economic expansion in member as well as non-member countries in the process of economic development; and
- to contribute to the expansion of world trade on a multilateral, non-discriminatory basis in accordance with international obligations.

The original member countries of the OECD are Austria, Belgium, Canada, Denmark, France, Germany, Greece, Iceland, Ireland, Italy, Luxembourg, the Netherlands, Norway, Portugal, Spain, Sweden, Switzerland, Turkey, the United Kingdom and the United States. The following countries became members subsequently through accession at the dates indicated hereafter: Japan (28th April 1964), Finland (28th January 1969), Australia (7th June 1971), New Zealand (29th May 1973), Mexico (18th May 1994), the Czech Republic (21st December 1995), Hungary (7th May 1996), Poland (22nd November 1996), Korea (12th December 1996) and the Slovak Republic (14th December 2000). The Commission of the European Communities takes part in the work of the OECD (Article 13 of the OECD Convention).

INTERNATIONAL ORGANIZATION FOR MIGRATION

IOM is committed to the principle that humane and orderly migration benefits migrants and society. As the leading international organization for migration, IOM acts with its partners in the international community to: assist in meeting the growing operational challenges of migration management, advance understanding of migration issues, encourage social and economic development through migration, and uphold the human dignity and well-being of migrants.

Pursuant to Art. 1.1(e) of the IOM Constitution, the purposes and functions of the Organization shall be: to provide a forum to States as well as international and other organizations for the exchange of views and experiences, and the promotion of co-operation and co-ordination of efforts on international migration issues, including studies on such issues in order to develop practical solutions.

The International Dialogue on Migration was launched at the IOM Council in November 2001 to provide a forum for IOM's 105 Member States and observer states and organizations to identify and discuss key issues and challenges in the field of international migration, with a view to enhancing understanding of and co-operation in migration. This seminar was one of the inter-sessional workshops of the International Dialogue on Migration.

Foreword

Since 2001, the Trade Directorate has undertaken work on the temporary movement of service suppliers under mode 4 of the WTO General Agreement on Trade in Services (GATS). Against this background, the Trade Directorate decided to focus its annual Services Experts Meeting, organised in co-operation with the World Bank, on the temporary movement of service suppliers under mode 4 of the GATS. Given the interest in bringing the trade and migration communities together, the meeting took the form of a seminar on trade and migration, held in Geneva and co-organised with the International Organization for Migration (IOM). The OECD Directorate for Employment, Labour and Social Affairs also provided input. The agenda for the seminar can be found in Annex I.1.

Mode 4, which has emerged as a major topic in the current WTO negotiations, raises a number of important and complex issues that go beyond the sphere of trade policy into the realm of migration policy and practices. The seminar responded to the need to build greater understanding of the opportunities and challenges related to mode 4 movement between the trade and migration policy communities. It represented an important opportunity for an informal exchange of views between trade and migration policy makers in a non-negotiating environment. The seminar brought together for the first time over 300 trade and migration officials from 98 countries and from a wide range of international organisations, as well as representatives of business and civil society.

The first two sessions of the seminar were chaired by Amina Mohamed, Ambassador of Kenya to the United Nations and Chair of the IOM Council. The third session was co-chaired by John Martin, Director of the OECD Directorate for Employment, Labour and Social Affairs, and Carlos Primo Braga, Senior Adviser to the World Bank. The last two sessions were chaired by Anders Ahnlid, Deputy Director-General of the Swedish Ministry of Foreign Affairs.

Participants exchanged views around three main issues. First, they explored the relationship between trade and migration, situating GATS mode 4 in the broader context of temporary labour migration. In this context, they looked at existing schemes to facilitate temporary movement at the national, bilateral and regional levels and asked what lessons could be drawn from these schemes for GATS mode 4. Second, they addressed issues relating to the management of mode 4, and of temporary labour migration more broadly, in both receiving and sending countries. Finally, they investigated what progress might be achieved in the current GATS negotiations and potential areas for future work.

This publication comprises three main elements. Part I contains the summary of the seminar's three days of presentations and highlights of the ensuing discussions. This report was prepared by Massimo Geloso Grosso and Daria Taglioni of the Trade Policy Linkages Division under the oversight of Dale Andrew, Head of the Trade Policy Linkages Division, and Julia Nielson, Senior Trade Policy Analyst, all of the OECD Trade Directorate. Part II comprises the background papers prepared for the seminar, which set out the major issues in the trade and migration debate addressed in the seminar. These were prepared by Julia Nielson, with input from Claire Inder, Maire McAdams, Heikki Mattila, Frank Laczko and Michele Klein Solomon of IOM and Daria Taglioni of the OECD. Part III contains a few concluding remarks on ways forward in the continuing building of bridges between the trade policy and migration policy communities prepared by Julia Nielson, Aaditya Mattoo (World Bank) and Michele Klein Solomon (IOM). Annex A provides a brief introduction to the GATS and mode 4 drafted by Julia Nielson and Daria Taglioni. Annex B is a short note on the difficulties of measuring mode 4 by Julia Nielson and Daria Taglioni.

This volume is published on the responsibility of the Secretary-General of the OECD.

Table of Contents

Acronyms

ACIP	American Council on International Personnel
APEC	Asia-Pacific Economic Cooperation
ATM	Automatic teller machine
CARICOM	Caribbean Community
CSME	CARICOM Single Market and Economy
DDA	Doha Development Agenda
ENT	Economic needs test
FDI	Foreign direct investment
GATS	General Agreement on Trade in Services
GATT	General Agreement on Tariffs and Trade
ICT	Information and communication technology
ILO	International Labour Organisation
IOM	International Organization for Migration
ISCO-88	International Standard Classification of Occupations
IT	Information technology
LDC	Least developed country
MFN	Most favoured nation
MRA	Mutual recognition agreement
NAFTA	North American Free Trade Agreement
ODA	Official development assistance
OFW	overseas Filipino worker
POLO	Philippines overseas labour office
Provisional CPC	United Nations Central Product Classification
RTA	Regional trade agreement
SMEs	Small and medium-sized enterprises
SPV	service provider visa
TBEP	Temporary Business Entry Program (Australia)
TN	Trade NAFTA (visa)
W/120	Services Sectoral Classification List (MTN.GNS.W/120) (WTO)
WTO	World Trade Organization

Part I

Trade and Migration

Report of the Seminar

Executive Summary

As part of the annual series of OECD Services Experts Meetings, the Trade Directorate, in co-operation with the World Bank and the International Organization for Migration (IOM), organised a seminar on trade and migration. Input was also provided by the OECD Directorate for Employment, Labour and Social Affairs. For IOM's membership, this seminar was the second inter-sessional meeting of IOM's International Dialogue on Migration and contributed to the dialogue's goal of enhancing understanding of migration and facilitating international co-operation in its management. The seminar, which was held in Geneva on 12-14 November 2003, focused on the temporary movement of service suppliers under mode 4 of the WTO General Agreement on Trade in Services (GATS). It brought together for the first time trade and migration officials from 98 countries and from a wide range of international organisations, as well as representatives of business and civil society.

Mode 4, the temporary movement of people to supply services, has emerged as a major topic in the current WTO negotiations and raises a number of important and complex issues that go beyond the sphere of trade policy into the realm of migration policy and practices. The seminar responded to the need to build greater understanding of the opportunities and challenges related to mode 4 movement between the trade and migration policy communities. It represented an important opportunity for an informal exchange of views between trade and migration policy makers in a non-negotiating environment.

The agenda of the seminar was structured around three main issues. First, it explored the relationship between trade and migration, situating GATS mode 4 in the broader context of temporary labour migration In this context, the meeting looked at existing schemes to facilitate temporary movement at the national, bilateral and regional levels and asked what could be drawn from these schemes for GATS mode 4. Second, it addressed issues relating to the management of mode 4, and temporary labour migration more broadly, in both receiving and sending countries. Finally, the meeting explored what progress might be achieved in the current GATS negotiations and potential areas for future work.

The debate on mode 4 is taking place against the backdrop of significant worldwide migration. Although some short-term signals indicate a slowdown in migration, long-term factors suggest continued growth, especially for migration from low-income to high-income countries. Important structural determinants include increasing variations in per capita income among countries, differing demographic structures, ease of international communications and transport, converging educational levels and the globalisation of production processes. Today, there are an estimated 175 million international migrants, nearly 3% of the world's population.

While migration is on the rise, there is no comprehensive international legal framework governing the cross-border movement of people. International legal instruments aimed at promoting the protection of refugees and migrant workers and at combating smuggling and trafficking of persons exist. To date, however, states have been reluctant to undertake binding international commitments that limit their sovereign right to determine who enters and remains within their territories and under what conditions, although they increasingly recognise the need to facilitate certain types of movement. Movement associated with GATS mode 4 covers only a very small percentage of annual cross-border movements of people. Within the universe of migration, there is the subset of temporary migration, and within that subset, there is a further subset of employment- or labour-related migration. GATS mode 4 is limited to the temporary movement of service suppliers and constitutes a further sub-subset within labour-related migration. However, the precise boundaries of GATS mode 4 are not well-defined, and this lack of definitional clarity poses challenges for migration officials. Further, while the GATS is not an agreement on migration, the wider and more ambitious the scope of GATS mode 4, the more it enters the migration debate. Identifying the scope of mode 4 remains a major task, but a task on which some useful progress was made at this seminar.

As with other forms of liberalisation, greater labour mobility offers potentially significant global economic benefits. One study estimates that liberalisation of labour mobility to the level of 3% of the workforce of OECD countries could result in global welfare gains of up to USD 150 billion a year(Winters *et al.*, 2003). For developing countries, given their strong comparative advantage in labour-intensive services, liberalisation of mode 4 could lead to significant benefits. Increased trade via mode 4 can also lead to increased trade by other modes of supply, by facilitating inward and outward flows of investment as well as cross-border trade in services. Mode 4 is an important component of the remittance inflows which are of increasing importance to developing countries. Aware of the economic importance of mode 4 and of labour migration more generally, many countries of origin are establishing proactive government policies to leverage the skills and international comparative advantages of their populations. The Philippines, for example, has established an active policy of managing overseas labour migration. India is increasingly promoting linkages and complementarities among different modes of supply.

From the business perspective, global corporations want to be able to move personnel around as needed and may be more inclined to invest in countries that facilitate this. While national laws usually accommodate most mobility needs of global corporations, their implementation is not always rational or efficient and thus creates additional costs for companies. The focus on temporary movement is also confusing; companies tend to take a longer-term perspective with respect to highly skilled workers and want to facilitate international hiring.

Many destination countries also realise the benefits of temporary labour mobility and facilitate movement at the national, bilateral and regional levels. Such schemes provide valuable lessons for GATS mode 4. One key concern is that, while GATS commitments are binding, the needs of local labour markets fluctuate significantly. Governments often choose to maintain needed flexibility by committing under GATS to less than their current levels of access while implementing other measures at the national, bilateral and regional levels.

National schemes discussed in the seminar seek to balance the need to ensure border integrity with responsiveness to the needs of business. The emphasis is on facilitating entry for the highly skilled and streamlining related visa and work permit processes. The new security environment is posing challenges in this regard. The seminar also explored a number of schemes for facilitating mobility under regional trade agreements. These ranged from those that facilitate entry but do not confer any rights of access (*e.g.* the Asia-Pacific Economic Cooperation [APEC] Business Travel Card) to those that provide access for certain types of service providers (*e.g.* the North American Free Trade Agreement [NAFTA]) to more ambitious schemes covering freedom of movement for the highly skilled (*e.g.* the Caribbean Community [CARICOM]). Bilateral labour agreements have also proved effective in giving countries a high degree of flexibility for targeting specific groups, sharing responsibility for monitoring and managing the migration flows between countries of origin and destination and minimising the potential impact of foreign workers on nationals, *e.g.* by requiring parity in terms of wages and social insurance.

In promoting greater labour mobility, distributional consequences need to be taken into account, as some groups in society may be negatively affected by liberalisation. From a trade union perspective, mode 4 liberalisation has the potential to open the door to unregulated migration, with negative impacts on local employment, wages and conditions, especially for low-skilled labour.

There is also a range of specific migration concerns related to mode 4, including overstaying, brain drain and general social externalities, such as cultural and other integration issues and lack of respect for social and labour rights. The seminar found most of these concerns to be manageable, given the political will and appropriate policy responses. A number of countries are successfully combating overstaying by mobilising resources for monitoring and focusing on employer obligations in sponsored entry programmes. Sponsors need not only to ensure rights for employees, but also to be responsible for workers' return travel and to co-operate with government monitoring of employees. Employers need to know that there are sanctions if they are found in breach of the requirements.

Similarly, concerns about brain drain can be minimised through policies that foster social support and brain circulation and encourage migrants to return to their country of origin with their newly acquired skills and experience. Evidence from bilateral agreements suggests that the most sustainable temporary migration programmes are those that are appropriately regulated and enforced and also afford flexibility through economic and social incentives. Perhaps the most important incentive is the possibility for migrants to re-enter the receiving country in future for work opportunities. Improved administration of visas and policies on residency to allow for readmission of personnel also play an important role.

Better management of remittances can also be crucial for establishing an enabling environment for return, by helping to create opportunities in countries of origin and enhancing the welfare of receiving families. In this regard, programmes that support small and medium-sized enterprises (SMEs) in countries of origin can be particularly beneficial, as can the establishment of remittance-friendly fiscal rules or community funds. Co-operation between sending and receiving countries and co-ordination between trade and migration officials at the national level is the most effective basis for obtaining significant results in terms of migration control and management.

The GATS contains the first formal recognition by trading nations of the importance of the movement of natural persons in services trade. In spite of this, little progress has been achieved in this respect. In the seminar, it emerged that countries' limited use of mode 4 is partly linked to the already-mentioned lack of flexibility of GATS commitments in a context of rapidly changing needs, along with the complexity of the Agreement and the conceptual and terminology gap between GATS definitions and migration regimes.

Areas in which the possibilities for progress could be explored in the current round of the GATS negotiations include:

- Expansion of existing commitments, including sectoral commitments, and elimination of explicit barriers such as quotas and economic needs tests.

- Reduction of administrative and procedural requirements, including exploring the feasibility of a GATS visa. A GATS visa would clearly separate mode 4 entrants from permanent migrants and result in *i)* reduced administrative costs, faster processing and approval; *ii)* fees limited to administrative costs; and *iii)* better records of mode 4 trade. Building safeguards and employer sanctions into the visa would prevent abuse and ensure the temporary nature of mode 4 movement. Questions were raised about the costs of implementing the visa, whether mode 4 entrants were an identifiable group for migration purposes, and whether a GATS visa would be sufficiently attractive to business.

- Improvements in effective access via regulatory transparency. Suggestions included establishing "one-stop shops" for all relevant information on mode 4 entry, prior consultation on new regulations affecting mode 4, and provision of additional information among WTO members.

It was thought that in terms of categories of workers, progress might be most likely for intra-corporate transferees, business visitors and highly skilled contractual service suppliers. It was also suggested that it might be more difficult to make progress on foreign employees of domestic companies, given disagreements about their coverage under mode 4 and greater sensitivity about the potential impact of this group on the local labour market.

However, several concerns need to be addressed, and reflection and further work may be warranted in certain areas:

- Migration has historically been addressed at the national level, but the need for international co-operation in managing migration, for example to combat trafficking and facilitate labour migration, is increasingly recognised. Nonetheless, the time is not ripe for managing migration in the framework of an international treaty, and the WTO is not in any case the appropriate forum for a debate on migration. International dialogue on migration, in IOM's Council for example, is beginning to identify common and complementary interests in the more orderly movement of persons and should be encouraged. Also, certain issues relating to labour and migration, such as labour rights or social security issues, are best addressed in other international forums, such as the International Labour Organisation (ILO).

- The scope of mode 4 remains uncertain. Clarification would be useful, as would its relation to categories and concepts used in migration policy, such as the definition of "temporary" and the relationship between employment-based and contract-based temporary movement.

- Mode 4 is at present under-estimated in trade figures owing to measurement problems. The economic benefits of increased movement of temporary services providers are not well documented. Ongoing efforts at the international level to improve mode 4 statistics and to improve understanding of the welfare gains from mode 4 liberalisation, including in relation to movement among developing countries, should be supported.

- More work is needed to better identify the range of complementary policies required to manage the potential costs and reap the benefits of increased mode 4 liberalisation. These include: incentives to turn brain drain into brain circulation; leveraging mode 4 to increase other forms of trade; remittance management; and measures to manage the social and labour market impact of temporary foreign workers.

- Binding commitments under mode 4 pose challenges for regulators in migrant-receiving countries. It would be useful to explore possible mechanisms within the GATS that might assuage the concerns of migration regulators while still achieving the predictability afforded by GATS commitments desired by business. In this context, the idea of "soft bindings", *i.e.* periods of improved access which may or may not result in binding commitments, deserves further exploration.

- Other means of facilitating entry need further study, including ways to increase the transparency and user-friendliness of the relevant migration regulations and whether to build on existing schemes for managing temporary entry or to explore the development of a GATS visa.

- Bilateral labour agreements tend to cover lower-skilled workers and provide a possible avenue for dealing with such workers in the short term. However, bilateral agreements are not most favoured nation (MFN), may not be covered by MFN exemptions and, given their diversity, are not always business-friendly. It might be useful to examine how the GATS and bilateral labour agreements might co-exist in the short term.

- Qualification requirements is one of the most difficult areas and can have a significant impact on the temporary movement of personnel. It is necessary to explore how to promote greater recognition, including through the development of incentives for negotiating mutual recognition agreements (MRAs) and dialogue with the relevant professional groups.

- The capacities of many developing countries to manage migration are currently limited. To manage the movement of persons in order to reap maximum developmental benefits, it may be useful to increase technical co-operation and capacity building for migration managers in the developing world and to promote co-operation between countries of origin and destination.

Reference

Winters, A., T. Walmsley, K.W. Zhen and R. Grynberg (2003), *Liberalising Temporary Movement of Natural Persons: An Agenda for the Development Round*, Blackwell Publishing, Oxford.

Report of the Seminar

This report provides a detailed résumé of the issues raised at the seminar. Like the seminar itself, the report is structured around three main issues. First, it explores the relationship between trade and migration, situating GATS mode 4 in the broader context of temporary labour migration. Existing schemes to facilitate temporary movement at the national, bilateral and regional levels are explored, and the lessons that can be drawn for GATS mode 4 are examined. Second, issues related to the management of mode 4 and temporary labour migration in both receiving and sending countries are addressed. Finally, progress that might be achieved in the current GATS negotiations and potential areas for future work are explored. The seminar agenda is attached as an annex.

WHAT IS THE RELATIONSHIP BETWEEN TRADE AND MIGRATION?[1]

Chair: Amina Mohamed, Ambassador of Kenya to the United Nations, Chair of the IOM Council

Objectives and structure of the meeting

Gervais Appave, Director, Migration Policy and Research, IOM
Aaditya Mattoo, Senior Economist, World Bank
Julia Nielson, Senior Trade Policy Analyst, OECD

The main objective of the seminar was to bring the migration and trade communities together with a view to enhancing mutual understanding, in particular with respect to GATS mode 4, and to gain better insight into the

---

1. All speakers participated in their personal capacity. The views expressed are thus not necessarily those of their governments.

opportunities and challenges ahead. A second objective was to gain better understanding of how temporary labour movement is – and can be – managed in countries of origin and of destination. A third objective was to consider what can and cannot be achieved through the GATS and to identify where alternative forms of international co-operation may be necessary. A final objective was to identify areas where more research and capacity building are needed.

The structure of the meeting reflected these objectives, with sessions covering:

- The trade and migration context: understanding mode 4 as a subset of temporary labour migration, itself a subset of temporary migration.

- Realities of temporary labour migration: experiences at the national, bilateral and regional levels with schemes for facilitating temporary labour movement and lessons for mode 4.

- Managing the impact of temporary labour migration: issues that arise for countries of origin and destination and approaches to dealing with them:

  – Issues in countries of origin: turning brain drain into brain circulation, remittance management, leveraging mode 4 movement to promote other forms of trade.

  – Issues in destination countries: impact of temporary foreign workers on the labour market, social integration and security concerns.

  – Issues common to origin and destination countries: ensuring temporariness (the problem of overstaying and successful return incentives); policy co-ordination between origin and destination countries and at the national level among trade, labour and migration officials.

- The GATS and beyond:

  – Overview of the categories of workers for which progress might be made.

  – Possible mechanisms for facilitating movement under the GATS, such as a GATS visa.

  – Ways to increase effective access through improvements in regulatory transparency.

  – Possibilities for progress under the GATS in the short and longer term, and areas where progress may best be achieved outside of the GATS through the development of complementary or supporting policies.

Trade and migration contexts[2]

Temporary labour migration and GATS mode 4

What is the bigger picture in terms of the rise of temporary labour migration?
Manolo Abella, Chief, Migration Branch, International Labour Organisation

In spite of the many and increasing restrictions, migration has expanded hugely in the last decade. Over this period, growth in migration has been up to 17 percentage points a year in the OECD area, but increased growth has taken place in all regions of the world. Long-term factors (*e.g.* increasing variations in per capita income among countries, differing demographic structures, converging educational levels and globalisation of production processes) suggest continued growth although some short-term signals indicate a slowdown. Supply clearly exceeds demand. It has been estimated that, each year, half a million people enter the European Union and 300 000 enter the United States clandestinely. Moreover, intra-developing country flows are characterised by presumably high, but largely untracked, movements.

There are few legal, official doors open for temporary labour migration, and there are many obstacles, including restrictions on recruitment, visa requirements, police records and other security checks, certification of where and for how long a person works, and insurance requirements. Nevertheless, many doors are in fact used. While legal doors are largely meant to be revolving (*i.e.* people that enter the country are expected to leave after a given period), many people stay beyond the allowed period. Often both the temporary foreign workers and their employers want them to stay, the latter because of the higher costs (*e.g.* in terms of training) involved in cycling employees in and out.

The main characteristics of current flows of temporary labour migration are the following:

- *Geographic dimension*: The growth in temporary labour migration flows is highest among neighbouring countries, in particular if they have agreements with one another and are rich. Movement between developed countries is the most liberalised and often takes the form of movement within regions through special arrangements with neighbouring countries. Statistically, movement from developing to developed countries is significantly higher than movement among developing countries. However, the latter is badly documented and is presumably much higher than the statistics indicate.

---

2. For background, please see Annexes A and B.

- *Categories of workers*: Movement of highly skilled workers is the most liberalised, with flows growing very fast over the last five years. In the United Kingdom, for example, annual growth has reached 35%. However, the definition of highly skilled workers is very broad, encompassing categories as diverse as intra-corporate transferees, temporary guest worker programmes and student migration. Worldwide, 1.5 million students are registered in tertiary-level education abroad, and much of their mobility will eventually become labour migration.

Where does mode 4 fit in the broader context of temporary labour migration?
Georges Lemaître, Principal Administrator, Directorate for Employment, Labour and Social Affairs, OECD

A number of concepts need to be clarified to give precise meaning to mode 4 and, more generally, to temporary migration. In the first instance, a temporary permit cannot be equated with temporary migration and stay. In many countries a temporary permit does not necessarily mean temporary migration, and the type of permit is not a reliable indicator of the effective duration of stay in a host country. Furthermore, migration and permit regimes are very diverse, to the detriment of the international comparability of migration practices. Within the traditional OECD countries of large-scale immigration (Australia, Canada, New Zealand and the United States), there is a clear demarcation between temporary and permanent migration. Transfers from temporary to permanent permits are possible, but, in general, temporary permit regimes are intended to reflect temporary migration. Most other OECD countries have only temporary permits, which tend to evolve towards longer-term types of permit and eventually permanent residence. In these countries, early attempts to create purely temporary categories of workers, *e.g.* "guest workers", foundered and led to a policy change towards more or less systematic permit renewals.

Additional problems arise from the fact that countries have different criteria for residency. In terms of migration, elements used to define residency and residency rights include nationality, type of permit, definition of duration of stay and fiscal status. In terms of mode 4, the GATS does not specify when and under what circumstances a foreigner is to be considered a resident of the receiving country. Similarly, mode 4 creates ambiguity with respect to the status of multi-year service providers: are they to be considered foreign residents engaged in trade or residents who are part of the productive capacity of the host country? Finally, to the extent that, in GATS terms, there is a dividing line between residents and non-residents, it remains unclear whether this can be assumed to be the conventional threshold of one year, which is customarily used from a migration perspective.

The suitability of granting freer access through mode 4 should be assessed in light of experience with the integration of immigrants. In OECD countries, experience is mixed. Although employment-based migration does not involve any initial fiscal burden on the host society and has a positive track record, current experience with migration is not all positive. Aging populations are leading to durable structural increases in demand for foreign and foreign-born labour. Demand is matched by extensive supply in the developing world. However, host countries have significant difficulty in preventing illegal entries and overstaying and in fostering integration of the foreign and foreign-born population. In many host countries, the unemployment rates of foreign or foreign-born workers are significantly higher than those of the total labour force. Abuses of humanitarian channels entail costs for the host country, and asylum seekers and refugees experience important difficulties in integrating.

Questions that need to be addressed in a debate on trade and migration include: whether there is a need for freer access when there are generalised labour shortages in receiving countries; the suitability of mode 4 and other truly temporary schemes to address these labour shortages; the real aims of mode 4, *i.e.* whether it focuses on satisfying labour shortages in the context of overall employment or on promoting competitive market access in services provision; whether better access (*i.e.* faster processing of permits) also means freer access; the likelihood that firms will actually co-operate to ensure temporary stay, given their limited incentives to cycle employees in and out; the appropriateness of distinguishing services provision from "human capital transfers"; and the real value of entering into "binding" commitments under the GATS.

GATS and mode 4
Hamid Mamdouh, Director, Trade in Services Division, WTO

GATS mode 4 is part of the broader definition of trade in services under the GATS. The four modes of supply are designed to capture the complete range of situations in which a service may be supplied. They are based on the territorial presence of the supplier and the consumer of a service. Obviously, supply through modes 3 and 4 involves the cross-border movement of factors of production (capital and labour). Therefore, they depart from the traditional balance of payments scope of trade, defined as taking place between residents and non-residents. More specifically, mode 4 covers the supply of services via the presence of natural persons. It covers situations where a natural person temporarily resides in the territory of the "export market" *for the purpose of supplying the service*. Thus, mode 4's coverage of migration is only incidental to the supply of a service. In such situations, the natural person involved could either be an employee of a service supplier (*e.g.* director or executive of a bank) or could be the service supplier proper (*e.g.* lawyer, accountant or software specialist).

The GATS defines mode 4 as "the supply of services via a service supplier of one Member to another Member through the presence of natural persons of a Member in the territory of any other Member". Service suppliers can be juridical persons employing physical persons from the home country or can be independent service suppliers selling their services to residents of another country. Hence, two main categories are covered by the GATS: employees of a juridical person and the self-employed, or contractual service suppliers. From a migration point of view, these categories are dealt with in completely different ways. The Annex to the GATS defines the outer limit of mode 4, stating that it does not apply to permanent employment, residency or citizenship. Governments are free to regulate in compliance with GATS principles, *i.e.* members are free to regulate migration provided that this does not nullify or impair their GATS commitments.

However, because the GATS covers all services sectors, mode 4 liberalisation may raise a broader range of domestic regulatory issues than would normally be addressed in a labour mobility agreement. This overlapping of competences requires an effort at co-ordination at both the national and international levels. The existence of a conceptual and terminological gap between GATS definitions and migration regimes creates difficulties for implementing provisions under mode 4 trade. Although mode 4 is not a migration category or concept, it is regulated by migration policies. While mode 4 issues will not determine overall policy on migration, because the GATS is an international treaty its 148 members have to find a way to integrate its legally binding provisions into the broader migration policy picture.

Because of the binding nature of GATS commitments, WTO members have tended to make limited concessions: commitments on mode 4 tend to be restrictive. Most mode 4 commitments are horizontal (*i.e.* not specific to individual sectors) and mainly target employees of juridical persons (93% of total commitments), while coverage of independent suppliers is scant (1% of the total). The overwhelming majority of commitments on mode 4 are linked to mode 3 (investment) and very few liberalise mode 4 as a stand-alone mode.

In spite of the narrow scope and limited commitments under mode 4, the reality of temporary movement of service providers is much bigger, and the schemes used are many and varied. The key reason for managing the temporary movement of service suppliers through alternative channels is the lack of flexibility of the GATS and mode 4 in a context of rapidly changing needs. Another reason may be the lack of consultation between national regulatory frameworks on trade and migration.

Today, a number of difficult questions remain unanswered, including how to reflect commitments in domestic legislation. Nonetheless, in the current negotiations, there are signs of a more concrete approach, with efforts at streamlining administrative procedures and increasing transparency and predictability. WTO members are increasingly trying to address the conceptual and terminological gap between GATS definitions and those of migration regimes. There is also a new tendency towards sector-specific commitments, a more clearly defined scope of commitments, and more disaggregated and better defined categories for entrants. Similarly, WTO members have demonstrated their willingness to identify multilateral criteria for addressing long-standing and controversial issues, including economic needs tests (ENTs) and labour market tests. Other initiatives aim at strengthening disciplines on mutual recognition agreements (MRAs) and studying the feasibility of a GATS visa.

Discussion

Many questions concerned the impact of GATS mode 4 on migration policies and on its application in specific cases. It was explained that, so far, there has been no demonstrable impact of WTO agreements on migration policies and that it was unlikely that GATS mode 4 would interfere with overall migration policies, given the very limited scope of GATS mode 4. However, there was considerable confusion owing to the fact that migration regulations do not use the same definitions as GATS mode 4. The distinction between service suppliers and generic job seekers was also explained. Job seekers are people seeking access to the employment market regardless of sector, while service suppliers normally enter to provide a specific service in a given sector (*i.e.* they have a contract for the delivery of a service upon entry). Mode 4 suppliers can therefore be defined in terms of both duration (temporary) and purpose (specific provision of services in a given sector) of stay. It was also clarified that the WTO does not deal with temporary migration more generally because this involves many policy issues that lie beyond the jurisdiction of the organisation.

The key challenges: what is at stake, trade and migration perspectives

Trade perspective: what is at stake for developing countries?
Lakshmi Puri, Head, Division on Trade in Goods, Services and Commodities,
United Nations Conference on Trade and Development

Mode 4 is an area where developing countries stand to make clear gains, and greater concessions under mode 4 can contribute a needed element of balance to the GATS. Progress on mode 4 serves as a test of progress towards equity of treatment among countries at different levels of development, by allowing developing countries to exploit their natural comparative advantages in international trade, including in labour as a factor of production. It also allows the world production system to achieve greater equity and balance between capital and labour flows. Furthermore, mode 4 can play a facilitating role, allowing developing countries greater access to international trade through linkages with other modes of supply. Mode 4 also contributes to poverty alleviation and to reduction of gender inequalities, as demonstrated by the positive gender impact and overall positive welfare effect of trade in nursing services.

Remittances are also good indicators of developing countries' interest in mode 4 trade. Officially, remittances are estimated at USD 72 billion worldwide (2001/02), but unofficial estimates suggest that the real value is double or triple this figure. Remittances are very important for both household consumption and the domestic economy and, in countries such as India and Sri Lanka, they exceed the economic value of the main export.

However, there are many challenges. First, mode 4 is a very sensitive area because of social, employment and migration issues as well as, more recently, security considerations. Negotiations and procedures are lengthy, slow and very bureaucratic. Improved statistics would provide a more solid basis for analysis and policy guidance and for a more dispassionate, concrete approach to negotiations. Second, greater efforts should be made to clearly separate temporary and permanent migration and to reduce the share of unilateral, discretionary systems that regulate temporary movement. Third, it is necessary to move away from the perception that mode 4 means migration and to build an orderly and predictable system for mode 4 movement. The perception that mode 4 leads to job losses must be demystified by pursuing sectoral and inter-modal analysis. Finally, the present level of mode 4 commitments needs to be improved, and dialogue between trade and migration communities is vital for disseminating information about the potential gains for both developing and developed countries.

Migration perspective: what are the channels through which international movement of service suppliers is easiest?
Philip Martin, Professor of Agricultural and Resource Economics, University of California, Davis

The way forward for mode 4 movement lies in linking it to mode 3 trade (commercial presence). Fundamental features of the relationship between trade and migration could, if better understood, help policy makers to identify the appropriate channels for achieving greater movement of service suppliers.

One important issue is fear about the manageability of migration flows originating from mode 4 liberalisation. Whereas 80% of trade in goods and services takes place between rich countries, mode 4 opens up movement from lower-income countries and unleashes fears about migration which reduce the likelihood of swift progress in liberalising the movement of people across borders.

Furthermore, trade and migration negotiating mechanisms differ, and reconciling them is very difficult. In trade, negotiations are structured so as to grant progressive and continuous liberalisation; in migration, policy measures are taken in response to observed needs.

A third issue arises from the inconsistency between the requirement of "temporariness" for mode 4 service suppliers and government and international organisations' efforts to grant and/or qualify equality of treatment for migrants (in terms of potential permanent migration). Differences between poor and rich countries are a motivating factor in international migration, and managing mode 4 implies the need to discriminate to keep "temporariness" effective.

Finally, building developing countries' capacity in mode 3 could theoretically facilitate services exports via mode 4. Most services trade is carried out via mode 3, and the best access conditions are given to mode 4 suppliers linked to mode 3 (*i.e.* those who are employees of juridical persons, rather than contractual service suppliers). Given that the immediate prospects for additional legislation on the movement of independent service suppliers via the GATS or breakthrough advances in mode 4 are low, if the ultimate goal is to move more people, efforts should aim at helping developing countries set up more subsidiaries of their domestic firms as a way to move service providers.

Discussion

A number of participants took issue with the proposal that developing countries should focus on increasing their ability to establish subsidiaries abroad. Many noted that scarce capital resources in developing countries suggest that obtaining mode 4 movement via mode 3 was a theoretical possibility but not an effective short-term solution. It was also observed that there is a compelling need to focus on the scope of mode 4. The broader its interpretation, *i.e.* to include a wider range of temporary and low-skilled labour (*e.g.* in agriculture), the more the debate is enmeshed with issues of general migration policy. However, it was observed that, while GATS mode 4 could pose real challenges for migration authorities, GATS is a binding treaty and countries are obliged to find ways to implement their commitments through their national legislation.

What is the reality in terms of temporary labour migration? What lessons can we learn for mode 4?[3]

National schemes

What approaches have countries taken at the national level to manage temporary labour migration? How do they fit with GATS mode 4? What have been the strengths and weaknesses of these initiatives? What lessons can we learn?

In this session, the national systems of the United Kingdom and the United States were presented. Both countries are significant receivers of various types of temporary entrants, and both systems are characterised by constant efforts to refine domestic migration policies and procedures.

Case study 1: United Kingdom
Nicholas Rollason, Solicitor, Kinglsey Napley

In the United Kingdom, the management of migration is very transparent, and all relevant information is easily accessible on the government Web site. An important characteristic of the system is the frequent consultation with stakeholders which ensures a very open and flexible framework that is responsive to market needs. Requirements for obtaining a work permit are very basic: a degree, an equivalent qualification or three years experience for the job on offer. Temporary and permanent migration flows are dealt with in the same way, so that immigrants entering with a temporary permit can apply for residency. Approximately 25% of temporary entrants become residents. Service suppliers tend to return to their country of origin more often than other categories of workers.

The categories of entrants covered under mode 4 include intra-corporate transferees, managers, business visitors and contractual workers. Special regulations apply to entertainers and artists. Schemes for low-skilled labour are clearly temporary, and there are a number of sector-specific schemes, *e.g.* for food processing, manufacturing, catering and seasonal agriculture.

The United Kingdom had initially foreseen a dedicated track for GATS mode 4 entrants but found that it lacked flexibility and results were unsatisfactory. Moreover, the objectives of GATS mode 4 could be attained via other means, and the flexibility that characterises the UK system allows existing schemes to be adapted to changing needs. For example, allowing foreign students to switch to work permits and to enter the British job market

---

3. For background, please see Part II, Chapter 1.

was a clear policy decision to meet current national needs and policy objectives aimed at using the expertise created to the best advantage of the United Kingdom.

In sum, the strengths of the system are its consultative, transparent, flexible, rapid and business-oriented character. The remaining challenge is to convince the public of the economic advantages of such an open system.

Case study 2: United States
Philip Martin, Professor of Agricultural and Resource Economics, University of California-Davis

Traditionally, the United States' infrastructure for migration policy has been very flexible. However, the United States is about to move away from the flexibility and proliferation of schemes on which it had depended until very recently. The increased security concerns of the last few years have added to the strain caused by the existence of large communities of immigrants, non-immigrants (foreigners who are expected to leave the United States after a period of study or work), and non-authorised migrants.

The US system includes a number of different schemes and takes into account various modalities of entry: through "front doors" as legal immigrants, through "side doors" as non-immigrants (with 18 types of doors with various levels of transparency, size and criteria), and through "back doors", or clandestinely. Since the terrorist attacks of September 2001, there is a strong determination to maintain people in the category under which they entered the country. Previously, once they were in the United States, foreigners could adjust their status from non-immigrant (student, guest worker) to immigrant or from unauthorised to immigrant status. This was very common, as shown by the fact that 85% of the economic employment visas issued each year used to be granted to foreigners already in the United States.

H1-B permits are the main gateway for moving professionals into the United States. While the current Congressional quota for H1-B permits is 65 000, numbers expanded enormously in the late 1990s, with business petitioning for increases of up to several hundred thousand permits. However, the atmosphere has changed radically in the last few years. In 2003, for instance, free trade agreements with Singapore and Chile that granted these countries a certain quota within the unchanged overall ceiling of 65 000 H1-B permits generated a plethora of protests both within Congress and from outside groups (mainly unions), arguing that trade should not affect migration policy. In the new climate, it is unlikely that the United States will create new doors for temporary entry of foreign workers in the near future, for instance by creating a GATS visa.

Bilateral labour agreements

> What kinds of agreements exist? What has been their purpose and what types of workers (e.g. skill level and sector) do they cover? How do these compare with GATS mode 4? What have been the strengths and weaknesses of these initiatives? What lessons can we learn?

This session discussed experiences with bilateral labour agreements concerning low-skilled workers in one country of origin (Honduras) and one destination country (Germany). Bilateral agreements in these countries have led to the orderly management of migration and related policies such as health and social security.

Case study 1: Honduras
German Leitzelar, Minister of Labour, Honduras

The upward trend in emigration observed in Honduras in the last decades has been sustained by strong push factors. In 1998, hurricane Mitch destroyed 80% of the country's infrastructure, magnifying existing structural weaknesses. With a 40% unemployment rate and more than 60% of the active population earning less than the minimum wage (USD 128 a month), the government has designed a new national strategy for facilitating exports of labour. Important changes in the national labour legislation have brought more flexibility into schemes regulating the mobility of unskilled workers.

Following this reform, Honduras put in place several initiatives aimed at securing strategic alliances with important partner countries. Honduras recently agreed the Seasonal Agricultural Worker Programme with Canada, through which Honduras sends rural workers to Canada for five to eight months. A second successful scheme covers the temporary employment of Honduran crew in shipping companies from Greece, Italy, Netherlands, Norway, Spain and the United States. From 2000 to 2002, 12 255 sailors were hired as contractual workers on foreign vessels for periods varying from six to ten months. A third bilateral scheme seeks to regularise illegal Honduran migrants to the United States and allows regularised workers to stay there legally for up to 18 months. This is an important programme for Honduras; it improves the working and social conditions of its population employed abroad as well as providing a source of capital in a country where 25% of the population lives on remittances from relatives abroad.

Case study 2: Germany
Torsten Christen, Federal Ministry of Economics and Labour, Germany

Germany has a number of bilateral agreements, mostly with central and eastern European countries, that cover seasonal workers, guest workers, border commuters and contract workers. All bilateral agreements are subject to wage parity conditions (*i.e.* a requirement to pay wages equal to those paid to German nationals). The three most important types of workers are seasonal workers, guest workers and contract workers.

Seasonal workers mainly work in agriculture and the hotel and restaurant industry. Current regulations allow work for a maximum of three months a year. This is the largest category; in 2003, Germany had more than 300 000 seasonal workers, most of them for the maximum of three months. Of these, approximately 250 000 came from Poland and about 20 000 from Romania.

Guest worker agreements normally cover exchanges of up to one year. The inflow of guest workers – a term derived from the German word *"Gastarbeiter"* – has been historically very important for Germany, which recruited millions of workers, mainly from Turkey, for its post-World War II economic revival. However, the programme is no longer very large.

Contract worker agreements have been signed by Germany with 12 central and eastern European countries and with Turkey. These agreements include country-specific quotas and enable employees of foreign companies to work in Germany as contract workers. The foreign company acts as a subcontractor of a German company, and the contract workers remain subject to the national legislation of their employer. The scheme is subject to a labour market clause and to a regional market clause. According to the labour market clause, national quotas are adjusted to meet market needs; according to the regional market clause, some regions in the eastern part of Germany are not allowed to employ foreign contract workers owing to high local unemployment rates.

From a migration perspective, Germany's experience shows that it is important to take into account the specificities of the market situation when designing labour migration policies. Similarly, it is important to guarantee transparency and rapid response. A new law being discussed in the German parliament proposes, among other innovations, to substitute the current dual approval procedure required for limited employment stays with a "one-stop shop" where work and residence permits are granted via an internal consent procedure.

What has been done to facilitate labour mobility at the regional level?

What kinds of schemes exist? What kinds of workers (e.g. in terms of skill level or sectors) are covered by these arrangements and how does this compare with GATS mode 4? What have been the strengths and weaknesses of these initiatives? What lessons can we learn?

This section describes three types of schemes operating pursuant to regional agreements: the APEC Business Travel Card, the NAFTA provisions for temporary entry of business visitors and the CARICOM framework for labour mobility. The three schemes take different approaches to regional labour mobility. While it is difficult to compare the agreements, they range from systems that do not provide access *per se* but facilitate the movement of certain groups by minimising migration procedures attached to their movement (the APEC Business Travel Card), to agreements that provide access for certain categories of service providers (NAFTA), to more ambitious schemes covering general freedom of movement for the highly skilled (CARICOM).[4]

Case study 1: The APEC Business Travel Card
David Watt, Department of Immigration, Multicultural and Indigenous Affairs, Australia

The APEC Business Travel Card was not intended for the GATS, but it covers very similar territory. Its story is one of balance between the integrity of national borders and the need to simplify procedures to boost competitiveness and trade among APEC member economies. While maintaining border integrity, the APEC Business Travel Card facilitates trade by reducing the costs and delays of bureaucratic procedures. It does so by simplifying short-term entry arrangements for business visitors, by streamlining processing for highly skilled workers seeking temporary residence and by ensuring transparent regulatory arrangements that allow for seamless cross-border movement.

When the programme was initiated in 1997, only three APEC members tried the card (Australia, the Philippines and Korea). A few other countries joined in 1999 as they recognised the benefits and as their capacity and confidence in the scheme increased. By 2003, the scheme covered 15 countries. The success of the APEC Business Travel Card is due to a range of factors including: its pathfinder approach, which recognises the different capacities of the economies and allows them to join when they are able to do so; the initial extension to a very limited number of countries in order to prove viability; an open and co-operative method which boosts confidence about the card's operational strengths; technical assistance schemes designed to aid

---

4. APEC's 21 members are: Australia; Brunei Darussalam; Canada; Chile; People's Republic of China; Hong Kong, China; Indonesia; Japan; Korea; Malaysia; Mexico; New Zealand; Papua New Guinea; Peru; Philippines; Russia; Singapore; Chinese Taipei; Thailand; United States; and Vietnam. NAFTA is the North American Free Trade Agreement between the United States, Canada and Mexico. CARICOM is the Caribbean Community consisting of 15 members and five associate member countries. The 15 members are Antigua and Barbuda; the Bahamas; Barbados; Belize; Dominican Republic; Grenada; Guyana; Haiti; Jamaica; Montserrat; Saint Lucia; St. Kitts and Nevis; St. Vincent and the Grenadines; Suriname; Trinidad and Tobago. The five associate members are Anguilla, Bermuda, British Virgin Islands, Cayman Islands, and Turks and Caicos Islands.

participating developing countries to implement the agreement successfully; a technology that requires deliberately low resources while ensuring robustness; and, finally, equal treatment of all participating countries.

Benefits for cardholders include a pre-clearance mechanism for short-term entry to participating economies with a single application (no need to apply separately for visa or entry permits for each entry), a scheme for multiple short-term entries (60-90 days per stay with overall card validity of three years) and fast immigration clearance on arrival and departure through preferential APEC lanes at major airports.

Participating APEC member economies benefit mainly from the consistency of approach for temporary business entry and from a double vetting procedure according to which business visitors are checked first by their country of origin and then by destination countries. Furthermore, countries maintain the right to control movement through borders and retain control over the eligibility of domestic applicants for the scheme.

Case study 2: NAFTA entry for business visitors
Paul Henry, Trade Policy Advisor, Economic Policy and Programs, Citizenship and Immigration, Canada

NAFTA aims to increase economic growth and living standards and to strengthen rules and procedures for regional trade and investment. It has a top-down and negative list structure for trade in services (*i.e.* unlike the GATS, all sectors are included unless they are specifically listed as excluded). The agreement covers citizens of NAFTA countries and is wider than the GATS in covering movement related to manufacturing and all investment. The NAFTA mobility scheme applies to business visitors, traders, investors, intra-corporate transferees and professionals.

Prior to NAFTA, the normal process of admission for temporary entry for non-NAFTA applicants involved two basic regulatory hurdles: labour market tests and a work permit. Additional obstacles included requirements for prior approvals and petitions, labour certifications and numerical restrictions. The NAFTA provisions for temporary entry eliminated or reduced these hurdles. Business visitors are no longer required to hold work permits while traders, investors and intra-corporate transferees need permits, prior approval and petitions but do not have to provide labour certification or undergo other procedures and are not subject to numerical restrictions. Professionals only need work permits.

The system introduces elements of harmonisation while ensuring faster processing for professional and business people by extending US immigration regulations to seven Canadian airports. Moreover, to date, it has not presented major contentious issues or problems for most travellers. However, the system has some weaknesses. It is rigid, complex and opaque and lacks provisions regarding lengths of stay, processing times and other elements of transparency. It is also very difficult to expand its coverage to other categories of workers. Finally, while many business people are aware of its existence, they wrongly assume that it will solve all their problems.

Case study 3: CARICOM
Madhuri Supersad, Director, Research and Planning, Ministry of Labour and
Small and Micro Enterprise Development, Trinidad and Tobago

The CARICOM framework for labour mobility is shaped on the European Union (EU) model. The CARICOM Single Market and Economy (CSME) seeks to merge its 15 member states into a single, enlarged economic entity as near to a single market and single economy as possible but does not envisage political integration. It is intended to provide an open market without cross-border restrictions and therefore to facilitate the free movement of final products, goods, labour and services.

The free movement of people is a critical factor. The treaty on the CSME abolishes discrimination on the grounds of nationality in all member states, granting professionals and their families – spouses and immediate dependents – the right to move freely within the CSME area.

CARICOM regulations for the movement of natural persons concern the free movement of skills and service suppliers, the right of establishment and the facilitation of travel. Mode 4 is seen as an additional global labour market tool that can help to attract more highly skilled and medium-level skilled service providers from outside the CARICOM region and thus contribute to equilibrium in the labour market.

At present, the CARICOM framework covers university graduates, artists, musicians, media workers, sportsmen and suppliers of services but coverage is expected to increase in accordance with the CARICOM plan of full removal of internal barriers envisaged for 2005.

CARICOM member states need to respond to a number of challenges in order to promote free movement. They need to improve administrative infrastructure and procedures and to harmonise labour regulations and standards. They must assist national and regional decision makers with studies on the impact of liberalisation on national labour markets. They have to adopt a regional approach to human resources development, *e.g.* by establishing a Caribbean association of national training agencies with a regional certification body and national bodies.

MANAGING MOVEMENT

Chairs: John Martin, Director, DELSA, OECD

and

Carlos Primo Braga, Senior Adviser, World Bank

Managing the impact of temporary foreign workers on countries of origin and destination[5]

Issues in destination countries: labour market, social and security issues

> *What is the impact of temporary foreign workers on the labour market of receiving countries and does the impact of mode 4 service suppliers differ? What is the impact, if any, of temporary foreign workers, including mode 4 service suppliers, on the pay and working conditions of nationals? What is their impact on unemployment? What is the relationship between availability of temporary foreign workers, including mode 4 service suppliers, and the trend towards contracting out of services? What are the social impacts of mode 4 service suppliers and how does this differ from other kinds of migration? How has the new security climate affected movement?*

Trade union perspective
Marion Hellmann, International Federation of Building and Woodworkers

Trade unions have important concerns regarding the possible disruptive social implications of allowing the free movement of temporary foreign workers, particularly in relation to the risk of social dumping and abuse of working conditions. Liberalisation under the GATS and enlargement of the European Union are important challenges as they will considerably increase cross-border mobility of workers.

---

5. For background, please see Part II, Chapter 2.

Mode 4 liberalisation has the potential to open the doors to unregulated migration, especially if future negotiations address facilitating movement of low-skilled workers. Many definitions used in the GATS are confusing, ambiguous and subject to interpretation: What is a manager? What is a specialist? Is a plumber a specialist? Furthermore, definitions and characterisations change from country to country. Finally, outsourcing, subcontracting and the existence of triangular relationships (*i.e.* between principal contractor, intermediary and employee) are potential threats to the enforcement of social conditions because the attribution of responsibilities and liabilities, the application of labour legislation and the functioning of the overall social security system become less accountable.

Examples of the negative effects of the liberalisation of labour mobility include:

- In Iceland, 600 Portuguese construction workers were hired by labour agencies for Italian principal contractors to build a dam and a tunnel. They reported poor medical assistance, non-compliance with health and safety standards, bad food and 16 hours of work a day paid at EUR 6 per hour.

- In Germany, an agreement between the social partners reduced the minimum wage in the former East Germany to allow firms to compete with firms from eastern Europe.

The way forward should be based on five guiding principles:

- The movement of labour should be regulated by labour legislation and social protection legislation, not by trade agreements.

- Visa and work permit problems are best solved bilaterally – on a case-by-case basis – or by regional agreements. The multilateral level grants too little flexibility.

- Movement of labour regulated by GATS mode 4 should only take place if it is linked to one of the other modes of supplying a service, never as a stand-alone mode.

- Mode 4 workers must be subject to national legislation, prevailing collective agreements and international conventions ratified by the host country. The results of mode 4 movement should be assessed at country level by all social partners.

- Abuse of mode 4 should be sanctioned.

Employer perspective
*Lynn Shotwell, Legal Counsel and Director of Government Relations, American
Council on International Personnel (ACIP)*[6]

Global corporations tend to invest in countries that facilitate the global movement of personnel. From the company's perspective it is irrelevant whether this happens through a GATS visa or by other means. Mode 4, as it is now, is perceived as insufficient to meet the needs of global corporations. The focus on service suppliers is only incidental to the operations of global corporations, and attention to temporary movement is perceived as confusing. From the corporation's perspective, all workers are permanent workers and multinational corporations want to be able to move them around as needs arise.

When a corporation needs to move people, it is confronted with migration systems. While national laws usually accommodate most mobility needs of global corporations, their implementation is not always rational or efficient. This can create real costs for companies – in terms of paperwork, penalties when contracts are broken because personnel were not in place in a timely manner, or productivity losses due to employees' anxiety about their unclear status. As current schemes for the movement of people only partly meet the needs of multinationals, they use alternative channels. For example, intra-corporate transferees are often placed on a permanent visa to allow spouses to work and to facilitate integration in destination countries. Even temporary visa schemes for professionals can be problematic. The H1-B visa scheme requires the employer to pay social security and other charges according to the local legislation, thus entailing duplication of costs for multinationals which have their own global compensation package.

Governments should adapt their mobility schemes to meet the needs of four employment groups:

- *Temporary business entrants:* workers that move abroad for less than six months without family. The biggest obstacles for this category of workers are delays in obtaining visas and permits. This type of worker usually needs to move on less than two weeks' notice. While this category could be dealt with using existing business visas, some problems could also be handled via the GATS.

- *International assignees:* includes junior staff moved around for training purposes or senior personnel moved to oversee projects. From a corporate point of view, an executive is an executive in every country. However, national legislation and definitions are different from country to country.

---

6. The ACIP is a trade association of large multinational companies dedicated to facilitating the international movement of personnel.

GATS could help to harmonise this and other basic concepts across countries.

- *High-potential international hires:* top graduates or highly talented individuals who can bring significant intellectual capital to an organisation over time. Employers want them to be treated as intra-corporate transferees, without pre-employment requirements.

- *Shortage workers:* these workers are usually hired locally. From a corporate perspective, the GATS is not useful for this category.

Government perspective
Michael Cunniffe, Department of Enterprise, Trade and Employment, Ireland

Traditionally a country of high emigration, Ireland has recently become the preferred location for many multinationals' European or global headquarters. The Irish viewpoint is particularly interesting because it reflects the lessons learned in managing a system that moved from 70% unemployment to full employment and where work permits issued jumped from 6 000 in 1999 to 43 000 in 2003. Following some serious economic mistakes in the 1970s and 1980s, the economy recovered and experienced "jobless growth" in the period between 1987 and 1993. Since 1994, employment increased rapidly to full employment and beyond, triggering a significant inflow of foreign workers.

The country's economic migration policy has been responsive to experience. Following a very large number of abuses, two categories of permits, intra-corporate transferees and trainees, were discontinued. The Irish immigration system is presently managed through three main instruments: work permits, working visas or authorisations and contract service suppliers. Another example of the system's responsiveness is illustrated by employment agencies. Economic migration has traditionally been vacancy-driven and illegal employment did not carry sanctions for employers. However, in the last few years, employment agencies have been responsible for several abuses, and the government changed the relevant legislation in April 2003. The feasibility of pre-clearance mechanisms for screening employers is now being studied.

An issue that has been widely debated in Ireland is whether permits and visas should be temporary or permanent. The immigration authorities are very attentive to both domestic and foreign experiences in managing migration. This led them to design a system that is formally temporary but can evolve towards more permanent arrangements. Job stability can, in fact, lead to eligibility for naturalisation. The impact on society has also been an issue of concern. Recent research suggests that lower pay in certain areas of strong immigrant employment may have helped to ease wage pressures. Concerns about abuses and pressures are still high because employers, guided by employment agencies, seek new and cheaper sources of labour. Other concerns hinge on assuring a minimum level of quality.

Balance is the real challenge: migration policy should be responsive and socially accepted. Flexibility and transparency are also important as part of achieving the goal of full employment. For example, because of labour shortages in construction, foreign workers have been allowed in this sector; however, if employment levels of national construction workers fall, this may be reviewed. GATS provisions could complement other immigration policies. One advantage of the GATS is that it addresses the employer, and this could be an important safeguard when dealing with contract workers.

Discussion

Many comments and questions reflected a lack of awareness about the needs of multinationals, while expressing interest in meeting some of their concerns. A number of participants sought clarification of the situation and working rights of family members accompanying temporary foreign workers. Family issues include employment rights for spouses, non-recognition of *de facto* couples and definition of the family unit. For example, child minders or grandparents are often not recognised as part of the family unit and hence denied the right to relocate abroad with the family. In Ireland, spouses can relocate with their partners provided that they have a job, while child minders can follow the family with a facilitated procedure provided that the person has lived with the family for at least 12 months. In response to a question on how the international community should best deal with family issues, it was answered that decisions should be taken at the multilateral level in order not to discriminate among employees; in many countries, for example, employees with a spouse of different nationality face more problems and bureaucratic processing than employees with a spouse of the same nationality. Others asked about the accessibility of information on immigration rules and procedures. From the perspective of the business community the problem was not access to information – nowadays facilitated by the Internet – but the implementation of laws in a non-transparent and subjective manner, unduly influenced by back-door politics. Finally, it was asked why mode 4 should be seen as posing different issues from the liberalisation of manufactures and the accompanying labour adjustment of the last ten years and why measures that are recognised as protectionist in manufacturing should be accepted in services trade as legitimate. The trade union position is that if there is capacity in the home country to provide a service, it should be provided domestically in order to preserve social stability.

Issues in countries of origin: remittances, brain circulation and broader trade linkages

> *How can countries best maximise the linkages between temporary movement and other forms of trade and growth (e.g. outsourcing or FDI)? What are the best practices in managing remittances?*

Promoting labour exports: the example of the Philippines
Maria Teresa Soriano, Executive Director, Institute for Labour Studies, the Philippines

As the world's top supplier of nurses, medical professionals and merchant marine crew, the Philippines is known as the "world's largest labour-exporting nation". In the last four years, the Philippines has deployed over 800 000 overseas Filipino workers (OFWs) who have sent home over USD 6 billion of remittances since 1999. The Philippines has over 1 400 agencies that recruit workers for overseas labour markets.

The Philippine government first adopted an international labour migration policy in 1974 as a temporary, stop-gap measure to ease domestic unemployment, poverty and a struggling financial system. The system has gradually been transformed into one of management of overseas emigration, culminating in 1995 in the "Migrant Workers and Overseas Filipinos Act", which put in place policies for overseas employment and established a higher standard of protection and promotion of the welfare of migrant workers, their families and overseas Filipinos in distress.

Currently, the government is actively exploring better employment opportunities and modes of engagement in overseas labour markets and promotes the reintegration of migrants upon their return. Instruments developed to this end include: pre-departure orientation seminars on the laws, customs and practices of destination countries; model employment contracts ensuring that the prevailing market conditions are respected and protecting the welfare of overseas workers; a system of accreditation of foreign employers; the establishment of overseas labour offices (POLOs) that provide legal, medical and psycho-social assistance to Filipino overseas workers; a network of resource centres for the protection and promotion of workers' welfare and interests; and reintegration programmes that provide skills training and assist returning migrants to invest their remittances and develop entrepreneurship.

The current debate hinges upon two issues:

- First, how deregulation and liberalisation will change the migration services of recruitment entities. Liberalisation, envisaged in the 1995 Act, foresees that the migration of workers will eventually be a matter between the worker and his/her foreign employer.

- Second, whether or not the government should shift its policy from "managing" the flow of overseas migration, which is reactive, to "promoting" labour migration, which is proactive. Such a shift would require including overseas Filipino workers in the national development agenda and the professionalisation of the deployment and even the qualification of these overseas workers. The entire system of training, deploying and securing Filipinos in overseas workplaces would be revised accordingly.

Dialogue and convergence of efforts at all levels among all stakeholders (government entities, private sector, destination countries, sending countries and migrants) are crucial to ensure adequate protection and welfare services to the migrants and to optimise the gains from overseas employment.

Links between mode 4 and other types of trade
Dr. Rupa Chanda, Associate Professor, Economics and Social Sciences, Indian Institute of Management, Bangalore

To date, GATS negotiations have tended to focus on individual modes. However, as there are real linkages between mode 4 and other types of services trade, countries should take a cross-modal approach to both domestic policy making and GATS negotiations to liberalise and facilitate trade and investment in services.

Services tend to be supplied simultaneously via several modes or in a phased manner through more than one mode of supply. Services trade can be embodied in information and data flows, financial flows, human capital flows or in goods, and can be subject to numerous policy constraints and technical and infrastructural barriers. In recent years, trade in services has been characterised by growing interdependence across modes of supply owing to the globalisation of production, economic liberalisation and technological advances. These factors have made possible trade in many previously non-tradable services and justify a cross-modal approach to understanding services trade and policy options. An integrated perspective on services trade can help to identify appropriate domestic policies and international strategies to enable leveraging of cross-modal trade opportunities in services.

Mode 4 facilitates inward and outward flows of capital via skill and technical transfers, development of specific knowledge, facilitation of networks and overseas contacts, access to funding, reputation effects and risk mitigation. The Indian information technology (IT) sector is an example of this.

The relationship between mode 4 and mode 1 is instructive. Despite the common perception that modes 4 and 1 are substitutes, the nature of their connection actually depends upon the level of specialisation and the nature of the services traded. In general, mode 4 leads to mode 1 trade and mode 4 can be important at all stages of mode 1 trade, but mode 1 can change the frequency, duration and level of mode 4 movement, including allowing for a shift to higher level personnel.

Substitutability takes place mostly at the low end of the specialisation chain (*e.g.* a call centre). Even here, there is scope for mode 4 trade, as mode 1 often requires the temporary presence of senior managers from the outsourcing company to determine requirements or other personnel to conduct training. Further along the value chain, the relationship becomes more complex. For instance, a company may be involved in sending its professionals to provide on-site services. Over time, once it has acquired a reputation and its activities are well-established, the company may set up subsidiaries (mode 3).

This presence in overseas markets and the exposure resulting from movement of service providers may also induce foreign direct investment (FDI) in the home country of workers. The credibility and viability of Indian expertise and the abilities acquired by Indian IT specialists working in the United States have induced FDI in India's IT sector by US multinationals. Thus, movement of labour may induce movement of capital, both inward and outward. The reverse may also occur, with the setting up of commercial presence (mode 3) followed by staffing of the overseas establishment with home country service providers (mode 4), possibly in a managerial capacity. Likewise, commercial presence in a country (mode 3) can create opportunities to export various services through outsourcing and electronic delivery to the source country of the investment or even to third countries (mode 1).

Particularly important in the success of the Indian domestic IT industry has been the role of the diaspora. Returning professionals have helped tap diaspora networks and make them aware of opportunities for doing business with Indian firms or starting a business in India. Indian professionals who have worked abroad have helped to establish and manage subsidiaries of global corporations in India.

Domestic policies and international strategies need to recognise the complementary relationship that exists across the different modes of supply. If governments take an integrated approach, a virtuous self-sustaining momentum can be created in services trade which clearly results in a positive sum game for exporting and importing countries. Mode 4 can play a central role in generating this momentum.

There are two broad areas for domestic policy action to maximise inter-modal linkages. First, governments must address the domestic, policy-based infrastructural and other constraints affecting trade in mode 4 and other modes. These include investing in quality education and training, establishing minimum standards and quality control across sectors, and enhancing the overall market competitiveness of the domestic service sectors. Second, they must increase the effectiveness of the main channels by which mode 4 influences the other modes, namely return migration, diaspora investment and openness to FDI.

Discussion

Participants asked about the resource requirements of the policies followed by the government of the Philippines. In the Filipino experience, resources for the management of migration have been limited. Costly training in specialised areas, including medicine and nursing, is managed by setting aside part of the revenue from overseas workers. In terms of how other countries can emulate the positive experience of India in leveraging the interlinkages between mode 3 and mode 4, it was explained that India was at first unaware of the interlinkages between modes of supply, and ways of attracting emigrants back to India are only starting to be developed. Nonetheless, the interlinkages were the result of a proactive government policy that leveraged the skills of a highly educated workforce. To a large extent, exports through mode 4 to the United States have been facilitated by the existence of H1-B visas.

Managing remittances
Alberto Islas, Technical Co-ordinator Director, Banco del Ahorro Nacional (Bank of National Savings and Financial Services), Mexico

The management of remittances in Mexico, particularly in relation to the US Hispanic migration population, clearly concerns a group that is much broader than the services providers covered by mode 4. Mexico is the second largest remittances market worldwide after India, accounting for almost USD 10 billion and growing at a rate of 30% in 2003. Not only has the number of Hispanics in the United States grown, but their GDP per capita has also increased. Electronic transfers dominate the remittance market, followed by money orders, while transfers of cash and personal cheques are relatively insignificant.

The cost of sending remittances from the United States to Mexico is composed of a service fee and the exchange rate and has been declining, although the market could be more efficient. The price of the service is set in the originator's network, which includes US remittance agents, banks and credit unions, as they determine the price and the exchange rate that is applied. The remittances are then collected in Mexican distribution networks, including banks, post offices and convenience stores. There is room for lower prices given the scale and growth of the market and technological innovation in financial services.

Under the "Partnership for Prosperity", the US and Mexican governments have undertaken several initiatives to provide a more secure and competitive service to migrants. These include endeavours to: *i)* increase the number of citizens using formal financial systems and to promote competition and innovation in these institutions; *ii)* improve transparency in the system, so that consumers are aware of relevant information, including prices, before they undertake a transaction; and *iii)* link remittances to access, through different savings mechanisms, to Mexican government programmes like housing and medical insurance.

Maximising brain circulation
Reynald Blion, Director, International Migration and Media Programme, Institut Panos, Paris

A key issue in labour mobility is to maximise brain circulation and ensure that it can benefit the public in both receiving and sending countries. Immigration in industrialised countries is inevitable because of demographic change and, if it is appropriately managed, it can benefit both origin and receiving countries. It is important to recognise that migration involves a complex set of issues relating to transfers of knowledge, skills and culture. For instance, while receiving countries can benefit from the knowledge and competencies of migrants, the latter may also return to their countries of origin with new skills and knowledge acquired abroad. In addition, further benefits may result from migrants' immersion in receiving countries' policies and culture. The experience and ideas that migrants take back to their countries of origin can play an important role in the development of these countries.

There are a number of ways to maximise brain circulation, including:

- Improve the administration of visas, *e.g.* greater flexibility regarding length of stay, which may be insufficient for certain projects if stays are too short.

- Design and implement better policies on residency, *e.g.* flexibility for re-admission of personnel who may need to return to the originating country to undertake or finalise a project and then go back to the receiving country.

- Increase the economic, social and political rights of migrants in both sending and receiving countries.

- Invest in information technology tools as competencies and knowledge can also circulate via the Internet.

- Promote migrants' participation in the development of their country of origin, *e.g.* establish programmes that enable migrants to return for given periods of time to their home countries to share their acquired knowledge in both the private and public sectors.

Discussion

The presentations raised several questions and comments, particularly from representatives of developing countries. Most interventions stressed that remittances are a very significant source of income for many developing countries, and that there is a need to better manage them in order to decrease costs and enhance the welfare of receiving families. In this regard, programmes that help to set up and operate small and medium-sized enterprises (SMEs) can be particularly beneficial for the well-being of families in receiving countries, given that SMEs comprise most of the businesses in developing countries. Other ideas for managing remittances include the establishment of community funds in the countries of origin or the possibility of giving migrant workers the choice to preserve their remittances in the currency of the host country, to avoid problems of currency devaluation. One participant asked about the effects of mode 4 on the Mexican *maquiladoras* (free trade zones). In reply, it was pointed out that, given the recent economic downturn, particularly in the United States, the *maquiladoras* have experienced decelerating growth and a decrease in labour movement, so that the impact of mode 4 is difficult to assess. It was also stressed that remittances came from a much larger group than mode 4 workers (*e.g.* remittances were also sent from permanent migrants and those working in sectors other than services) so that care should be taken in using remittances as a measurement of mode 4 trade. At present, it is not possible to break down remittances to isolate the proportion coming from workers who would fall under GATS mode 4.

Ensuring temporariness: overstaying and return incentives

How can countries of origin and destination co-operate to prevent overstaying? What kinds of schemes have been successful in promoting return migration? What are the problems? What are the links between temporary and permanent migration?

Australia's Temporary Business Entry Program
David Watt, Department of Immigration, Multicultural and Indigenous Affairs, Australia

For governments, ensuring temporariness is a matter of choice; it is possible to keep temporary movement temporary, but it may not always be viewed by the governments concerned as being desirable to do so.

There are considerable economic benefits, including increased trade and investment, to facilitating the movement of business people. Australia's Temporary Business Entry Program (TBEP) responds to business needs and enables businesses to bring personnel into Australia quickly. However, this is balanced with the need to ensure local employment and border integrity.

Because Australia is a mature economy, employment opportunities are in capital- and knowledge-intensive industries. Therefore, the TBEP is for skilled professionals, managers and technical personnel, for whom the local employment rate is relatively high. The system includes a business visa for short stays (for negotiations, meetings, etc., not remunerated in Australia) and for long stays. The latter requires sponsorship by the prospective employer and can provide for up to four-year periods of stay. It includes only skilled occupations which are paid at or above a minimum specified salary level.

In both cases the overstay rate is very low at 1% or 2%. Australia ensures temporariness in the following ways:

- *A universal visa system.* This allows quick immigration clearance as passenger details are known before arrival. Databases also make it possible to identify people who do not leave when their visas expire.

- *Focus on skills.* Long-stay applicants must have managerial, professional or technical skills, which are in demand worldwide.

- *Employer obligations.* Sponsors must, besides ensuring certain employee rights, such as award-level wages or responsibility for medical costs, be responsible for workers' return travel and co-operate with the government's monitoring of employees.

- *Monitoring and compliance.* Sponsors are regularly monitored and can be sanctioned if they are found in breach of the requirements. The sanctions range from bans on sponsorship to financial fines. To date, compliance rates have been very high.

Dealing with overstaying
Ms. Irena Omelaniuk, Director of Migration Management Services, IOM

There are serious concerns in receiving countries about labour migrants who stay beyond the duration of their contracts. Other concerns relate to the fact that if migrants are sent back and encounter very difficult conditions they will find other ways to try to access the global labour market. Labour programmes that provide secure return arrangements, for example by allowing re-entry to the receiving country for future work opportunities, are more likely to help stabilise movement.

Ensuring return can be greatly facilitated by the social networks maintained in the country of origin and can be essential to: *i)* increase the perception in the global community of good governance in the sending country and of orderly regulation of migration by the receiving country; *ii)* bring significant dividends for countries of origin; *iii)* return newly acquired skills/experience to contribute to development and growth of the country of origin; and *iv)* increase confidence in liberalised forms of labour movement. However, governments often give little attention to the issue of return, perhaps because of a lack of international experience in the labour field or of resources to monitor and enforce return.

The temporary movement of workers increasingly takes place through bilateral labour agreements. A noteworthy characteristic of bilateral labour agreements is that they allow for the temporary movement of unskilled labour, a group largely excluded from current scheduled GATS commitments on mode 4.

There is a clear distinction between the conditions offered to skilled and unskilled workers in receiving countries. The former are likely to enjoy the most favourable residence status, and it is with respect to these workers that the distinction between temporary and permanent migrants is increasingly blurred. By contrast, unskilled labour migration programmes seek to treat the migrants as temporary guests and to preclude their integration, in an effort to ensure their return.

However, evidence from some bilateral agreements suggests that the most sustainable programmes are those that are appropriately regulated and enforced but also afford flexibility through economic incentives and social support. Perhaps the most important incentive is to allow migrants to re-enter the receiving country in future for work opportunities, including the possibility of receiving higher wages if the migrant comes for a second time or is personally nominated by the employer. Enforcement is best ensured through regulations that involve employers in the process and sanction employers who do not honour their commitments.

Governments in the home countries of temporary labour migrants can also help by establishing an enabling environment for return. For example, some countries have created a climate of opportunity through fiscal rules whereby remittances are not taxed. Other countries have incentive schemes as part of diaspora management strategies, such as loans to support small businesses for returnees and diaspora. Finally, the exchange of information and co-operation between sending and receiving countries can lead to significant results in this area.

Policy co-ordination

> *How can we promote greater policy co-ordination between countries of origin and destination and between trade and migration officials at the national level? How can we ensure stakeholders' involvement?*

Sandro Siggia, Deputy Director-General, Italians Abroad and Migration Policies, Ministry of Foreign Affairs, Italy

Since the 1980s, Italy, which had previously been a land of emigration, has become a land of immigration. In view of increasing public concerns about the growing number of immigrants, Italy began to adopt new mechanisms to cope with this phenomenon.

Italy's immigration policy is based on the assumption that it is not possible to obtain significant results in terms of migration control and management without the co-operation of the sending countries. Also, policies should reflect the needs of the economic system and the country's scope for absorbing foreign labour. Useful instruments include:

- Electronic systems able to identify demand from industry.

- Professional training schools for foreign workers in Italy or the sending country.

- Agreements with foreign countries for selection of workers in particular skill categories.

- Offices for the assistance of foreign workers in Italy.

- An "observatory on migration" aimed at improving knowledge of migration.

- Agreements with foreign countries on temporary migration.

Italy has negotiated a number of bilateral labour agreements. Mechanisms to facilitate return include:

- Readmission agreements, which lay down the conditions and procedures for identifying and repatriating illegal immigrants. These are often linked to development assistance agreements.

- Programmes linking economic assistance to the progress of sending countries in implementing policies to prevent trafficking and exploitation of human beings and to combat criminal organisations.

- Schemes linking a country's quota of work permits to its record on facilitating return of its nationals.

It is essential to encourage immigrants to maintain links with their countries of origin in order to protect their cultural identity and to facilitate their reintegration in their societies, with their increased financial resources, know-how and often a more business-oriented mentality. In this regard, particular care should be taken to ensure productive management of remittances.

Policy co-ordination within Italy is undertaken by the Ministry of Labour, which handles requests from the different Italian regions. The regions receive requests for labour (skilled, seasonal, permanent workers, etc.) from local employers. The Ministry of Labour then establishes the total number of workers needed during the year and allocates quotas to selected foreign countries. This operation is undertaken in co-ordination with the Ministries of the Interior and of Foreign Affairs.

Shahidul Haque, Regional Representative for Southern Asia, IOM

Trade, development and migration are inextricably linked, although migration seems to have been excluded in the current phase of globalisation. Trade and migration can reduce poverty through several channels, including the creation of employment, reduction of the vulnerability of families, and exchange of knowledge.

A framework for co-operation between the trade and migration policy communities should be established and there should be greater awareness of the links between them. The framework should include origin and destination countries in order to deal appropriately with the difficult issues involved. Regional arrangements and relevant international organisations also have an important role to play.

At the national level, migration should be mainstreamed into development planning. A national programme approach (programme-based migration management) could include the following strategy: *i)* government-led country-wide needs assessment to ascertain the situation, priorities, needs and concerns; *ii)* a plan of action for the implementation of assessment recommendations; and *iii)* capacity development of individuals, institutions and societies in an integrated manner.

Discussion

Some participants stressed that there is no "one size fits all" approach to managing migration. Different models need to be applied in different situations to allow for flexibility and to respond better to labour market needs. Others argued that migration is inevitable and that it is therefore advisable to put in place a framework that will ensure that it occurs in an orderly, predictable and humane manner. International agreements can play an important role; however, ways of improving co-ordination among organisations working in this area need to be found. It was also pointed out that countries already have a range of tools to eliminate or minimise problems resulting from migration, such as overstaying (*e.g.* imposing appropriate sanctions on employers). The possibility of drawing lessons from bilateral agreements was also mentioned, as was the issue of the compatibility of such agreements with the non-discrimination (most-favoured nation – MFN) requirement of the multilateral trading system. It was explained that, for trade in services, WTO members are allowed to deviate from the MFN principle under certain circumstances. For example, they may deviate from the MFN requirement in the case of regional trade agreements which meet the criteria of GATS Article V, and it is possible that labour arrangements that form part of these agreements may fall under the MFN exemption. Also, given the uncertainties about the scope of mode 4, certain types of bilateral labour agreements may not fall within the scope of the GATS; it could be argued, for example, that bilateral labour agreements for agricultural workers do not fall within the scope of the GATS as such workers are arguably not service suppliers.

PROSPECTS FOR THE GATS NEGOTIATIONS FOR MANAGING MOVEMENT

**Chair: Anders Ahnlid, Deputy Director-General,
Ministry of Foreign Affairs, Sweden**

Facilitating access under the GATS[7]

For which categories of workers can we make progress?

What are the issues arising for different categories of workers in terms of skills levels, duration of stay and nature of the contractual relationship (i.e. employment-based, contractual service suppliers, intra-corporate transferees)?

Adriana Suarez, Permanent Mission of Colombia to the WTO

There is increasing awareness of the benefits that liberalisation of mode 4 can bring both to industrialised and developing countries. Progress achieved in bilateral agreements, including with respect to different categories of workers,

---

7   For background, please see Part II, Chapter 3.

shows that there is scope for advancing these issues at the multilateral level. This would help to ensure that developing countries increasingly participate in the multilateral trading system and that progress is achieved in sectors and modes of supply of interest to them. It would also bring about benefits to industrialised countries, in particular with respect to the link between modes 3 and 4.

Three main areas are relevant to understanding the issues involved in relation to the different categories of workers under mode 4:

- *Progress achieved in the Uruguay Round.* The GATS Annex on mode 4 includes two main categories of workers: *i)* natural persons who are service suppliers of a member (or who are self-employed); and *ii)* natural persons of a member who are employed by a service supplier of a member. There is no mention in the Annex of any exclusion of service suppliers in relation to skill level. The majority of commitments on mode 4 are in the horizontal section of the schedules and very few members have made sector-specific commitments on mode 4. Most commitments concern intra-corporate transferees, business visitors and highly skilled labour in general. There are very few commitments for contractual service suppliers, in particular for independent service suppliers (*i.e.* not employees of a juridical person). The nature of the commitments has created a lack of balance *vis-à-vis* developing countries, which have a comparative advantage in independent service suppliers.

- *Categories of service providers contained in current negotiating proposals, requests and offers.* In the current GATS negotiations, several requests have been made concerning contractual service suppliers, in particular independent service suppliers in that category. A number of requests have also been made for sectoral commitments on mode 4. Some general negotiating proposals from the first phase of the negotiations also address the need to include independent service suppliers. However, only a few offers to date have proposed changes on mode 4, mostly in relation to intra-corporate transferees, trainees, specialists and contract-based services.

- *Concerns and areas where progress is needed.* Perhaps the most important concern relates to ensuring temporariness. However, this should be done at the national level by the migration authorities and not at the WTO. In order to take into account the interests of developing countries, progress needs to be achieved in the area of independent workers. There is also a need to make greater sectoral commitments on mode 4 and to decrease the administrative burden of visas and work permits. Progress on the issue of definition of categories of service providers under the GATS will also be important.

Martin Hirsbrunner, Lawyer, Swiss Federal Office for Migration/IMES

Swiss commitments on mode 4 from the Uruguay Round are substantial. They include several categories of highly skilled workers, such as managers, executives and intra-corporate transferees. There is a system of quotas, but there are no economic needs tests and no priority by nationality. Authorisations are issued by cantons and requests for entry are not generally submitted in relation to the GATS mode 4; workers are often authorised to enter the market without knowing about the existence of mode 4 commitments.

While the GATS is an agreement to facilitate and enhance trade and not a migration agreement, it is difficult to discuss mode 4 without becoming involved in the migration debate. The percentage of foreign workers in Switzerland is quite high, up to 20% of the total. Rules restricting foreign entry are in place mostly to ensure employment for Swiss nationals and to strike the right balance between foreign and domestic workers.

In terms of the GATS, the Swiss position is clear:

- Most labour migration schemes in Switzerland relate to highly skilled labour, with lengths of stay depending on the category of workers; programmes for low-skilled labour are not contemplated at this stage.

- For Switzerland, the definitions contained in GATS commitments relating to managers, specialists, etc., are sufficiently clear; it is also important to allow countries to maintain flexibility given the variety of approaches used.

- Switzerland's scheme, like the GATS, does not apply to the movement of persons seeking access to the employment market.

- A GATS visa seems neither necessary nor feasible from Switzerland's standpoint. Authorisation by the cantons is rapid, provided that certain conditions are met, and no special GATS visa is under consideration.

- Transparency is crucial to all parties involved. Laws, rules and regulations should be easily accessible, including via the Internet.

Mark Hatcher, European Services Forum

It is important for WTO members to work towards rebuilding the momentum for a successful round of negotiations. Businesses increasingly operate in international markets; if they cannot move their personnel around, their competitiveness is likely to be affected. Bilateral efforts play an important role in liberalising movement of mode 4 type workers but should not be a substitute for multilateral liberalisation under the GATS.

It is important, however, to be realistic about what can be achieved in the current round of talks. Overly ambitious goals, particularly in relation to low-skilled labour, may have a negative impact on the overall negotiations. It is probably better to address low-skilled labour in bilateral agreements, at least at this stage. Areas where progress can be achieved at the multilateral level include the following:

- Expansion of horizontal commitments for certain types of skilled workers instead of sectoral commitments, which may prove too difficult. These could include executives, managers, etc., but also people undergoing training and development at all levels.

- Improvement of issues of definition and classification, although it is important to allow flexibility, in light of the fact that categories of service providers may change over time (*e.g.* in the IT sector).

- Reduction of administrative burdens, which can unduly delay business operations.

- Enhancement of transparency, including in relation to the period of stay, information on which should be specific and easily accessible to the public.

The European Services Forum has developed a model schedule as a basis for focusing negotiations on the temporary entry of natural persons. It provides for ways to improve existing market access and national treatment commitments in the WTO for certain categories of service providers, calls for efforts to increase transparency and reduce procedural and administrative burdens relating to the movement of personnel, and foresees safeguards and penalties to protect against abuse.

Discussion

The discussion was lively. The importance of defining contract-based versus employment-based movement was raised by several participants; for example, contract-based service providers tend to have shorter stays and tend not to be entitled to the same social and labour rights in the receiving country. Some participants raised concerns relating to workers that attempt to change their status once in the country. However, other speakers reiterated the possibility of establishing safeguards to address such problems, *e.g.* not allowing visa holders to change categories, fines for non-compliance, exclusion from future schemes or monitoring. Participants also emphasised the importance of qualification requirements for professionals.

In response to a question on the current GATS provisions in relation to recognition, it was explained that the GATS permits recognition as an exception to MFN (*i.e.* WTO members can recognise qualifications or experience gained in some countries but not others) but does not require recognition to be granted. Further, the GATS does not require any particular approach to recognition or the use of any particular criteria. The main requirement is that WTO members do not discriminate in the application of their criteria for recognition (*i.e.* they can use whatever criteria they like, so long as they apply the same criteria to all members). Further, WTO members should notify recognition agreements to which they are a party to the WTO and give other interested WTO members the opportunity to negotiate to join those agreements or to negotiate a similar agreement if they wish (again, this is only a requirement to provide an opportunity for other members to show that they meet the required standards, but it is not a requirement to grant recognition).

Several developing country participants pointed out that progress on mode 4, to be useful to developing countries, must include low-skilled labour. A number of speakers reiterated that progress on low-skilled workers is probably unrealistic under the GATS at this stage, but that there might be more scope to make progress in this area under bilateral agreements.

What measures can be taken to facilitate movement under mode 4?

GATS mode 4 is a logical grouping from a trade perspective, but how does it fit with existing migration schemes? Can mode 4 be separated and treated differently from other kinds of temporary migration?

Sumanta Chaudhuri, Permanent Mission of India to the WTO

It is important to ease and streamline visa procedures and conditions for effective market access. Inefficient visa formalities, including lack of transparency, onerous administrative procedures and delays, might nullify or impair GATS commitments. A GATS visa would provide for less stringent conditions for entry and stay and would apply to both horizontal and sectoral commitments. Separate sets of conditions would apply for each category of workers, *e.g.* intra-corporate transferees, business visitors or contractual service suppliers (both juridical entities and independent professionals).

The visa would stipulate specific conditions, such as periods of validity, multiple entry or conditions for renewal. Furthermore, documentation requirements would be clearly laid down, related fees would reflect administrative costs, and deadlines, including in relation to documentation and appeal procedures in case of denial, would be clearly set out. Finally, in order to ensure temporariness, the visa would include safeguard provisions such as penalties for abuse and establishment of patterns of frequent misuse by companies.

Furthermore, the GATS visa represents a mechanism for achieving the separation of temporary movement under the GATS from permanent migration. Without this differentiation, the concerns of overall migration policy and security issues overshadow all other trade considerations for temporary movement under GATS.

Future research could, *inter alia*, usefully survey existing practices in member regimes, consider the administrative structures that would be needed to implement a GATS visa, and assess the potential costs and benefits involved.

Bimal Ghosh, Consultant to the IOM

The GATS is the first formal recognition by trading nations of the importance of movement of natural persons in services trade. However, little real progress towards freer movement of natural persons has so far been achieved. This is basically due to the confusion between the movement of service-providing persons and labour migration. It is important, therefore, to clarify the distinction between a service-providing person and a labour migrant. While the GATS provides for the movement of natural persons, regardless of their levels of skills, it explicitly excludes natural persons seeking access to the employment market of a member.

Greater liberalisation of mode 4 could bring significant benefits to all countries and in particular to countries at lower levels of development. Indeed, there is a wide range of services in which developing countries have a comparative advantage and mode 4 is key to the delivery of such services. Nevertheless, there are also problems that need to be addressed. These include the possible resistance of trade unions to the presence of large numbers of foreign personnel and body "shopping", under which professionals attached to a firm in a foreign country may be lent or subcontracted to a local firm.

Ideas on how to move forward include:

- Focus on deepening national commitments on freer movement of service providers in cases where the GATS provisions are clear. Attempts to overburden the GATS by bringing labour migration within its scope should be avoided.

- Focus on intra-company transfers, including placement of trainees; movement on the basis of service trade contracts between firms; and movement of self-employed professionals based on service trade contracts.

- In order to be of interest to both developed and developing countries, give consideration to "packages" that include both modes 3 and 4.

- Make better use of enquiry points to increase transparency.

- Be aware, and make better use, of the flexibility allowed by the WTO in scheduling commitments.

- Take advantage of regional and inter-regional MRAs.

- Pursue the idea of a special visa regime as a facilitating and monitoring tool.

- Encourage developing countries to take full advantage of assistance by relevant organisations.

Discussion

Several participants stressed the importance of streamlining administrative procedures for visas and work permits. Some questioned the feasibility of a GATS visa, suggesting instead that the framework could be used flexibly to design schemes that best suit local needs and conditions. Given the existence in some OECD countries of a range of schemes providing access for several different types of mode 4 entrants, it was noted that if a special GATS visa was to be attractive to business it would have to be faster, cheaper and easier than existing schemes. There was some speculation about whether this would be the case. Several speakers also questioned the feasibility of a new GATS visa from a security standpoint, particularly after the events of September 11, 2001. The importance of ensuring consistency between any new commitments and those made in the Uruguay Round was also raised, including to avoid backtracking, *i.e.* situations where the new negotiations actually resulted in reduced access.

Increasing effective access via regulatory transparency

What gains can be made in mode 4 access by increasing regulatory transparency? What sorts of improvements might be considered? What are the implications, including in terms of resources, for migration and trade authorities?

Paul Henry, Senior Policy Analyst, Economic Policy and Programs, Citizenship and Immigration, Canada

In the area of mode 4, transparency is vital. The business community is concerned because they find temporary entry laws, regulations, administrative procedures and guidelines complex and mysterious. The information currently provided by governments, although potentially useful, is often out of date or incomplete. This can be particularly problematic for SMEs, which generally lack the capacity to obtain the information they need.

Ensuring transparency also entails costs; it requires time, effort and resources. However, the resulting benefits may well offset the costs. For business, improved information means getting ready ahead of time, better planning and business strategies, and reducing the risks of doing business. For governments, administrative costs can be decreased and overall efficiency can be enhanced. Transparency can not only foster international trade and investment, it can also help countries better manage immigration issues, because they can more readily obtain and exchange information.

Mode 4 commitments, as currently spelled out, are difficult for business to understand, although they should be the main beneficiary of such commitments. Even negotiators do not always know how liberal their initial offers are. Canada has attempted to find ways to reduce these problems by tabling a proposal in current GATS negotiations for a complementary exchange of relevant information through bilateral processes. The results of such exchanges would then be shared with all the other members.

Lack of transparency means that it is hard for trade negotiators to convince the business community and other stakeholders of the benefits of liberalisation. More and better information on mode 4 can increase the value and priority of the GATS.

Discussion

One participant stressed the importance of transparency in facilitating business operations and increasing overall economic efficiency. Areas of particular concern identified include: i) the lack of specific criteria, e.g. in labour market tests, which leave scope for discretion; ii) the lack of clarity in, and the complexity of, schedules of commitments; iii) the lack of information on deadlines for applications; and iv) failure to provide information on reasons for refusal of applications. One area where progress could be made is in requiring countries to undertake prior consultation on new regulations affecting mode 4 (i.e. providing other WTO members with an opportunity to view and comment upon new regulations that affect trade in mode 4 before they are introduced). However, it was noted that this requirement might be administratively burdensome for countries at lower levels of development. There were also calls for improvement to existing notification requirements, allowing for more frequent and detailed provision of information. It was also remarked that further convergence in the definition of categories of services providers would also improve transparency. Other speakers emphasised the importance of transparency, including in relation to immigration laws and regulations. It was stressed that information needed not simply to be made available, but to be made more "digestible" so that is of greater use to business. One participant also raised the possibility of including additional information on laws and regulations in the schedules of commitments on a voluntary basis.

Where can we go from here?

> *What progress may be feasible in the context of the GATS negotiations? What are other ways to make progress? What policies are important in managing movement?*

Jan Karlsson, Chair, Global Commission on International Migration, Sweden

Trade, especially trade in services, and migration will continue to increase in years to come and it is important to keep the issues in a dynamic context. Projecting the issues under discussion into the future, some observations can be made:

- Current discussions focus on limiting the scope of the GATS, *e.g.* temporary versus permanent or certain skill levels. However, demographic changes in industrialised countries will mean that labour shortages will grow and that there will be an increasing need for foreign workers. Scarcity will mean that governments will put in place mechanisms to attract foreign workers.

- The categories of workers will also change in time so that although issues of definition and classification are important, there is also a need for flexibility; for example, IT service providers did not exist a few years ago.

- The gender aspect will increase in importance as there will be greater need for domestic and other services and movement of women is likely to increase.

- Although bilateral trade agreements can play an important role, they cannot be substitutes for the multilateral trading system. In future, there will also be a need to regulate migration at the multilateral level.

Alejandro Jara, Ambassador of Chile to the WTO and Chair of Services Negotiations

In terms of the current GATS negotiations, around 39 offers had been tabled so far, but many members still need to participate more actively in the process. In addition, the offers on the table so far generally represent a "standstill" exercise, in the sense that the commitments offered reflect an "existing" situation and consequently no new business opportunities are being created. This being said, it seems that in terms of mode 4 a few members have made some limited movement towards liberalisation.

While a number of developing countries had submitted requests and offers, more needed to be done to encourage and assist other developing countries to do so. There is also a need to strike a balance in the negotiations, so that both developed and developing countries can reap the full benefits of liberalisation. Equally, much remains to be done to demonstrate to the business community the potential benefits of liberalisation, and to encourage their more active involvement in the negotiations. Not unrelated to this is the need to make the system more user-friendly, including through increased transparency and public scrutiny. On mode 4, involvement of the migration policy community in the negotiations would obviously be central to making real progress.

Finally, while much of the current focus is on the market access negotiations, important negotiations on rules under the GATS are also in progress. There is still a lot of work to be done in these negotiations, which cover government procurement, subsidies, possible disciplines on certain types of domestic regulation and a possible emergency safeguard for trade in services.

Hamid Mamdouh, Director, Trade in Services Division, WTO

There are four main areas where progress needs to be made. First, there is a need to contribute to the policy debate, in particular on ways to reconcile the economics of liberalising trade under mode 4 with issues of migration, employment and security. Liberalisation can be beneficial if undertaken at the right pace and under the right conditions. Second, it is important to find ways to bridge the gap between the trade and migration communities. The GATS is a trade agreement which aims at increasing market access for service suppliers; how countries manage migration is for them to decide. Third, qualification requirements is one of the most difficult areas and can have a significant impact on the temporary movement of personnel. There is a need to develop mechanisms, such as mutual recognition agreements, to minimise problems relating to qualification requirements. Finally, better co-ordination at both the national and international levels is crucial.

Ms. Anya Oram, Directorate General Trade, European Commission

With mode 4, the GATS created an artificial concept which does not match the reality of migration. The question is how to adapt it to that reality, particularly since the GATS, as a WTO agreement, is here to stay. There are issues relating to labour and migration, namely labour rights, brain circulation and social security issues, that should not be dealt with in the WTO. These are very important issues that are better addressed in other forums such as the ILO. Governments should also ensure appropriate co-ordination at the national and international levels. In relation to the current round of negotiations, it is important not to raise expectations too high, particularly in relation to unskilled labour. At the same time, if there is the political will, a great deal can be achieved on mode 4. For example, the seminar has shown that overstaying is a problem that can be addressed.

Aaditya Mattoo, Senior Economist, World Bank

Several areas of interest have emerged from the seminar. As with other forms of liberalisation, there are potentially significant net economic benefits from greater labour mobility, but distributional consequences also need to be taken into account, as some groups of society will be negatively affected. In addition, there is a range of specific migration concerns including overstaying, social externalities such as lack of respect of social rights, cultural and integration issues, and security issues. Some remedial policies for these have been identified, *e.g.* in relation to overstaying, which seem to be manageable if there is the will to do so.

An important element of current negotiations relates to reciprocal liberalisation, *i.e.* countries have an incentive to move forward if they are tempted by improved market access in trading partners. Areas where progress can reasonably be expected include: *i)* elimination of explicit barriers such as quotas; *ii)* reduction of administrative and procedural requirements; and *iii)* improvements in the area of transparency.

However, there are also problems and concerns that need to be taken into account. With respect to coverage, focusing only on trade in services appears artificial, including in relation to the categories created in the GATS. Consideration should be given to whether there is a need to go beyond the GATS mandate – that is, beyond service suppliers – to better reflect the reality of temporary migration. Further, flexibility may be needed in relation to binding commitments, as these may curtail countries' ability to address cycles in the labour market and migration. In this context, the idea of "soft bindings", *i.e.* periods of generosity which may or may not result in binding commitments, deserves further exploration. Finally, in relation to skills, in order to ensure that the GATS is a genuinely multilateral agreement, improvements should be made in the area of semi-skilled labour. Co-operation between sending and receiving countries in relation to managing overstaying could prove very useful to this end.

Discussion

Several speakers stressed the importance of achieving progress on mode 4, in particular for developing countries. There was agreement on the importance of increasing co-ordination between the trade and migration communities at both the national and international levels, to address the complex issues raised during the meeting. The need to explore the synergy between bilateral initiatives and the multilateral trading system was also raised. It was suggested that further work could explore the south-south aspects, *i.e.* mode 4 and migration issues between developing countries.

Concluding remarks

Ken Heydon, Deputy Director, Trade Directorate, OECD

This kind of meeting is extremely useful for enhancing mutual understanding in the trade and migration fields. Although gaps in perception remain, there is now more transparency and better understanding between the two policy communities. In terms of what can and cannot be done by the WTO in the framework of mode 4, the GATS is not a migration agreement, as was mentioned several times in the course of the meeting. However, it also appears that the wider and more ambitious the GATS becomes, the closer it gets to the migration debate. In order to bring coherence to that debate, a number of key requirements were identified, notably involving greater transparency, clarity and flexibility, both within the GATS and in domestic regulations dealing with migration. Another important element of coherence will be to look at potential complementarities between the multilateral approach, via the GATS, and bilateral approaches, given that the latter, unlike the GATS, tend to cover unskilled workers. The bilateral agreements, however, tend not to be bound, are not MFN and, owing to their diversity, are not always business-friendly.

Three other areas of potential future work have been raised: *i)* improved understanding of the welfare gains from mode 4 liberalisation; *ii)* better understanding of the importance of binding commitments and the implications for the migration community; and *iii)* examination of the way in which the GATS and the bilateral agreements might co-exist.

Brunson McKinley, Director General, IOM

Both migration and trade will grow in years to come. This underlines the need for better co-ordination and co-operation between the two policy communities and for the continuing involvement of other stakeholders, including civil society, in the policy dialogue. A key area for current and future efforts at the practical level is capacity building for developing countries, to assist them to manage the challenges posed by demographic and economic changes and to harness opportunities for development. An important component would be building capacity for migration training in education and other government systems. Further work could also usefully focus in more detail on some of the key issues for migration policy managers, such as overstaying or managing remittances. Continuation of discussions such as this between the trade and migration communities is an important component of the overall effort to improve the management of migration at the international level to make it more orderly, predictable and safe and to reap its positive potential more widely.

Annex I.1. Agenda of the OECD/World Bank/IOM Seminar on Trade and Migration

Geneva, Palais des Nations, 12-14 November 2003

IOM International Organization for Migration
OIM Organisation Internationale pour les Migrations
OIM Organización Internacional para las Migraciones

THE WORLD BANK

12 November: What is the Relationship between Trade and Migration?
Chair: Amina Mohamed, Ambassador of Kenya to the United Nations, Chair of the IOM Council
Objectives and structure of the meeting
Gervais Appave, Director, Migration Policy and Research, IOM
Aaditya Mattoo, Senior Economist, World Bank
Julia Nielson, Senior Trade Policy Analyst, Trade Directorate, OECD
Session I: Trade and migration contexts
Temporary labour migration and GATS mode 4
What is the bigger picture in terms of the rise of temporary labour migration? Manolo Abella, Chief, Migration Branch, International Labour Organisation
Where does mode 4 fit within the broader context of temporary labour migration? Georges Lemaître, Principal Administrator, Directorate for Employment, Labour and Social Affairs, OECD
GATS and mode 4 Hamid Mamdouh, Director, Trade in Services Division, WTO
Discussion

The key challenges: what is at stake, trade and migration perspectives

Trade perspective: what is at stake for developing countries?
Lakshmi Puri, Head, Division on Trade in Goods, Services and Commodities, United Nations Conference on Trade and Development

Migration perspective: what are the channels through which international movement of service suppliers is "easiest"?
Philip Martin, Professor of Agricultural and Resource Economics, University of California-Davis

Discussion

Session II: What is the reality in terms of temporary labour migration? What lessons can we learn for mode 4?

National schemes

What approaches have countries taken at the national level to manage temporary labour migration? How do they fit with GATS mode 4? What have been the strengths and weaknesses of these initiatives? What lessons can we learn?

Case study 1: United Kingdom
Nicholas Rollason, Solicitor, Kinglsey Napley

Case study 2: United States
Philip Martin, Professor of Agricultural and Resource Economics, University of California-Davis

Discussion

Bilateral labour agreements

What kinds of agreements exist? What has been their purpose and what types of workers (e.g. skill level and sector) do they cover and how do these compare with GATS mode 4? What have been their strengths and weaknesses? What lessons can we learn?

Case study 1: Honduras
German Leitzelar, Minister of Labour, Honduras

Case study 2: Germany
Torsten Christen, Federal Ministry of Economics and Labour, Germany

Discussion

What has been done to facilitate labour mobility at the regional level?

What kinds of schemes exist? What kinds of workers (e.g. in terms of skill level or sectors) are covered by these arrangements and how does this compare with GATS mode 4? What have been the strengths and weaknesses of these initiatives? What lessons can we learn?

Case study 1: The APEC Business Travel Card
David Watt, Department of Immigration, Multicultural and Indigenous Affairs, Australia

Case study 2: NAFTA entry for business visitors
Paul Henry, Trade Policy Adviser, Economic Policy and Programs, Citizenship and Immigration Canada

Case study 3: CARICOM
Madhuri Supersad, Director, Research and Planning, Ministry of Labour and Small and Micro Enterprise Development, Trinidad and Tobago

Discussion

13 November: Managing Movement

Chairs: John Martin (Director, DELSA, OECD)
Carlos Primo Braga (Senior Adviser, World Bank)

Session III: Managing the impact of temporary foreign workers on countries of origin and destination

Issues in the destination countries: labour market, social and security issues

What is the impact of temporary foreign workers on the labour market of receiving countries and does the impact of mode 4 service suppliers differ? What is the impact of temporary foreign workers, including mode 4 service suppliers, on the pay and working conditions of nationals? What is their impact on unemployment? What is the relationship between availability of temporary foreign workers, including mode 4 service suppliers, and the trend towards contracting out of services? What are the social impacts of mode 4 service suppliers and how does this differ from other kinds of migration? How has the new security climate affected movement?

Trade union perspective
Marion Hellmann, International Federation of Building and Woodworkers

Employer perspective
Lynn Shotwell, Legal Counsel and Director of Government Relations, American Council on International Personnel

Government perspective
Michael Cunniffe, Department of Enterprise, Trade and Employment, Ireland

Discussion

Issues in countries of origin: remittances, brain circulation and broader trade linkages

How can countries best maximise the linkages between temporary movement and other forms of trade and growth (e.g. outsourcing or FDI)? What are the best practices in managing remittances?

Promoting labour exports: the example of the Philippines
Maria Teresa Soriano, Executive Director, Institute for Labour Studies, The Philippines

Links between mode 4 and other types of trade
Dr. Rupa Chanda, Associate Professor, Economic and Social Sciences, Indian Institute of Management, Bangalore, India

Managing remittances
Alberto Islas, Technical Co-ordinator Director, Banco del Ahorro Nacional, Mexico

Maximising brain circulation

Reynald Blion, Director, International Migration and Media Programme Director, Institut Panos, Paris
Discussion

Ensuring temporariness: overstaying and return incentives

How can countries of origin and destination co-operate to prevent overstaying? What kinds of schemes have been successful in promoting return migration? What are the problems? What are the links between temporary and permanent migration?

David Watt, Department of Immigration, Multicultural and Indigenous Affairs, Australia

Irena Omelaniuk, Director of Migration Management Services, IOM

Policy co-ordination

How can we promote greater policy co-ordination between countries of origin and destination and between trade and migration officials at the national level? How can we ensure stakeholders' involvement?

Sandro Siggia, Deputy Director-General, Italians Abroad and Migration Policies, Ministry of Foreign Affairs, Italy

Trade, development and migration
Shahidul Haque, Regional Representative for Southern Asia, IOM

Discussion

Session IV: Facilitating access under the GATS

For which categories of workers can we make progress?

What are the issues arising for different categories of workers in terms of skills level, duration of stay, nature of contractual relationship (i.e. employment-based, contractual service suppliers, intra-corporate transferees)?

Panel

Adriana Suarez. Permanent Mission of Colombia to the WTO

Martin Hirsbrunner, Lawyer, Swiss Federal Office for Migration/IMES

Mark Hatcher, European Services Forum

Discussion

What measures can be taken to facilitate movement under mode 4?

GATS mode 4 is a logical grouping from a trade perspective, but how does it fit with existing migration schemes? Can mode 4 be separated and treated differently from other kinds of temporary migration?

Sumanta Chaudhuri, Permanent Mission of India to the WTO

Bimal Ghosh, Consultant to the IOM

Discussion

Increasing effective access via regulatory transparency

What gains can be made in mode 4 access by increasing regulatory transparency? What sorts of improvements might be considered? What are the implications, including in terms of resources, for migration and trade authorities?

Paul Henry, Senior Policy Analyst, Economic Policy and Programs, Citizenship and Immigration Canada

Discussion

Session V: Where can we go from here?

What progress might be feasible in the context of the GATS negotiations? What other ways are there to make progress? What policies are important in managing movement?

Panel

Jan Karlsson, Chair, Global Commission on International Migration, Sweden

Alejandro Jara, Ambassador of Chile to the WTO and Chair of Services Negotiations

Hamid Mamdouh, Director, Trade in Services Division, WTO

Anya Oram, Directorate General Trade, European Commission

Aaditya Mattoo, Senior Economist, World Bank

Closing remarks
Chair: Anders Ahnlid
Deputy Director-General of the Swedish Ministry of Foreign Affairs

Ken Heydon, Deputy Director, Trade Directorate, OECD

Brunson McKinley, Director-General IOM

Part II

Issues for Trade and Migration

Chapter 1

The Reality of Temporary Labour and Mode 4 Movement

This chapter presents a variety of schemes to facilitate the temporary movement of labour at the national, bilateral and regional levels. While a number of these schemes cover workers beyond the scope of mode 4 – *e.g.* by including those in sectors other than services – their experience, strengths and weaknesses, can provide some valuable lessons for initiatives relating to mode 4 movement. Exploration of these schemes can also shed light on the question of how schemes more focused on mode 4 workers would mesh with existing regimes.

National schemes

Globally, temporary migration is on the increase. In many countries, the emphasis is on facilitating movement by the highly skilled, with governments devising new temporary migration schemes to respond to a range of factors, including skills shortages in the domestic labour market or the demands of large global companies looking both to recruit globally and to assemble global teams for specific projects at short notice. Some governments also see the ability to access the highly skilled on a global basis as a contribution to the international competitiveness of the economy as a whole.

In the late 1990s and the early 2000s, most OECD countries introduced special measures to facilitate the recruitment of highly qualified foreign workers, leading in many cases to increases in entrants (see Box 1.1).

While these schemes remain in place, it is unclear whether the same increases will be seen in the coming years. Some of the labour shortages in OECD countries are expected to increase, in part as a result of ageing populations (*e.g.* the demand for health and care workers, for which there is no substitute for human labour, is expected to continue to rise). However, in other areas, shortages have tended to fluctuate, particularly in the information and communication technology (ICT) sector where large shortages foreshadowed around 2000/01 are being revisited in light of the bursting of the dot.com bubble.[8]

Box 1.1. Recent increases in temporary foreign workers in OECD countries[9]

In the United Kingdom, the number of approved work permit applications increased from 85 600 in 2000 to 115 700 in 2001 (versus 58 200 in 1999). Increases were particularly high in key sectors such as education (100%), healthcare (nearly 42%) and computer technology (roughly 25%).

In Ireland, the number of work permits granted doubled between 2000 and 2001 to 36 400. This increase was concentrated in service sectors (*e.g.* in the healthcare sector permits increased up to 65%), but was not limited solely to sectors employing skilled workers (*e.g.* there were also significant increases in the hotel industry).

In Switzerland, the quota for skilled workers, which had been unchanged for over ten years, was temporarily raised in May 2001 by nearly 30% to meet labour market requirements.

In Korea, the number of documented skilled foreign workers rose from 17 700 in 2000 to nearly 28 200 in 2001, an increase of nearly 60%.

In Germany, the employment of foreigners tripled in the healthcare sector, and more than 13 000 foreign computer engineers obtained "green cards" under the programme instituted in August 2000, which foresees the issuance of "green cards" in accordance with the length of an employment contract, for a time period that may not exceed five years.

In the United States, the quota of highly qualified temporary visas (H1-B), which had been raised to 195 000, was not used up entirely in 2001, although more than 163 000 permits were distributed, representing an increase of more than 40% from the previous year. However, the quota is likely to revert to the legislatively mandated level of 65 000 for 2004.

Source: OECD.

These fluctuations are one of the reasons why the openness of national systems is not always reflected in GATS commitments. Indeed, while GATS commitments on mode 4 are limited (see Annex A, "A Quick Guide to the GATS and Mode 4"), they do not necessarily represent the existing level of

---

8. Measurement of labour shortages remains a challenge. Measurement methods differ greatly among countries and the reliability of many estimates is highly contested. The OECD *Employment Outlook* (2003) notes that when the broader concept of "non-employment" – encompassing both unemployment and inactivity – is taken into account, OECD countries appear rich in unused labour reserves.

9. While these are temporary entry schemes, visa- or permit-holders may be entitled in some cases to apply for permanent residence after a certain period. Applicants may be required to leave the country before applying however.

openness. This is a reflection of the fact that while GATS commitments are binding, the needs of local labour markets can fluctuate significantly, and governments often choose to maintain flexibility by committing to less than their current levels of access and by implementing some measures via national, bilateral and regional arrangements. Actual trade is thus much greater than GATS commitments would suggest.

Key questions

o   What are the types of categories of workers covered by national schemes to facilitate movement? To what extent do they go beyond the coverage of mode 4 (*i.e.* beyond service suppliers)?

o   What lessons can we learn from national systems to facilitate movement? What have been the challenges for such systems?

o   Who are the main stakeholders and what kinds of political management are involved in setting up such systems?

Bilateral labour agreements

Bilateral labour agreements serve a range of purposes. For the *destination country*, the primary aim is to address skill gaps in the local labour market, whether for seasonal workers or low-skilled labour or for more highly skilled workers in sectors such as health or ICT. Agreements can also be used to foster broader economic objectives; within Europe, bilateral labour agreements have been developed in harmony with the ongoing process of deep regional economic and monetary integration. They were used at first to assist the development of and, more recently, the enlargement of the European Union to include the acceding countries from central and eastern Europe. Bilateral labour agreements can also play a role in combating irregular migration. Providing a legal channel for temporary entry can reduce the incentives for illegal migration and contribute to securing the willingness of countries of origin to co-operate in managing irregular migration, including with regard to readmission of nationals (*e.g.* Italy signed both a labour and a readmission agreement with Albania in 1997). Cultural and historical ties may also play a role, as in the "Working Holiday Maker" programmes operating between the United Kingdom and some Commonwealth countries.

For *countries of origin*, bilateral labour agreements can be a means to increase their workers' access to international labour markets and to promote the enhancement of occupational skills, technology transfer and the development of their human capital. Agreements can also ensure that workers who have acquired new skills return to their country of origin, thereby avoiding "brain drain". For example, a proposed scheme between the Dutch and Polish Ministers of Health aims to prepare Polish nurses for employment in the Dutch healthcare system for a maximum period of two years and to facilitate their return and reintegration into the Polish healthcare system.[10] Finally, sending countries can use bilateral labour agreements to secure the rights and welfare of their workers abroad (the Philippines has signed a number of such agreements).

Bilateral labour agreements provide a high degree of flexibility for countries to target specific groups, adapt to fluctuating labour market conditions and share responsibility for monitoring and managing migration between sending and receiving countries. They can also contain provisions to minimise the potential impact of foreign workers on nationals, *e.g.* by requiring wage and social insurance parity (see Box 1.2).

Bilateral labour agreements tend not to be included in GATS commitments, for two reasons. First, they would not comply with the requirement that access offered to one WTO member must be offered to all other WTO members (the most-favoured nation, or non-discrimination, requirement). Indeed, a number of agreements are the subject of MFN exemptions under the GATS (see Annex A). GATS commitments are also guaranteed minimum treatment, so committing to such schemes under the GATS may deprive the host countries of the flexibility with which the schemes are currently implemented (Winters *et al.*, 2001).

Not all countries have entered into bilateral labour agreements. The vast majority of the US admission programmes are open to citizens of all countries.[11] The range of temporary visa programmes includes both skilled professionals (*e.g.* H1-B visas) and other kinds of temporary labour (*e.g.* H2-A, temporary agricultural workers). Ireland, aside from a longstanding arrangement with the United Kingdom and its participation in the European Economic Area,[12] does not have any substantive bilateral agreements with other countries. Working visas cover specified skilled occupations in designated categories; around 75% of work permits cover semi-skilled or unskilled workers, mostly in services (Sexton, 2003). The United Kingdom has also not concluded any major bilateral labour agreements in the last 40 years,[13] with most schemes open to global recruitment. The work permits scheme is geared towards the more highly skilled (university degree or equivalent

---

10. A letter of intent for this scheme, "Polish nurses in the Netherlands: development of competencies", was signed between the Dutch and Polish Ministers for Health in July 2002.

11. The exception is programmes for Canadian and Mexican nationals under NAFTA, outlined in the following section.

12. The EEA includes the EU countries plus Iceland, Norway and Liechtenstein.

13. Two new treaties on illegal migration have been signed with Bulgaria and Romania.

professional experience); other schemes exist for lower skilled and seasonal agricultural workers.

Box 1.2. Examples of bilateral labour agreements

Canada and the Caribbean and Mexican Seasonal Agricultural Worker Programme

The programme involves Canada and Jamaica, Mexico, Trinidad and Tobago, Barbados, Antigua and Barbuda, Dominica, Grenada, Montserrat, St. Kitts and Nevis, St Lucia, St. Vincent and the Grenadines. It operates in Alberta, Manitoba, Ontario, Quebec and Nova Scotia where it was introduced in response to shortages of available Canadian agricultural workers.

Before applying for migrant agricultural workers, employers are required to consider the availability of Canadians. If these are unavailable, employers submit an application specifying the number of workers required, the length and location of the work, and the working and living conditions. The employer can specify individual workers by name, but otherwise participating governments recruit and select the workers in the countries of origin, and work permit applications are processed by the local Canadian embassy or consulate.

The programme is strictly seasonal and workers can only stay in Canada for a maximum of eight months. The minimum term of employment must not be less than 240 hours in a term of six weeks or less. Employers are responsible for workers' return travel costs and for providing their accommodation at no extra charge and must pay them the highest applicable minimum wage. Workers cannot seek alternative or additional employment or transfer to another farm without government approval. Employers face sanctions (penalty of up to CAD 50 000 and/or two years' imprisonment) if workers enter the local labour market. The programme does not open any right of access to more permanent status.

Experience with the programme has generally been considered positive. The possibility of re-circulation, and the fact that workers coming for a second time or named by an employer benefit from higher wages and lower fees, has led to a smaller number of overstayers than in other similar programmes.

German Contract Worker Scheme

This scheme operates between Germany and a number of countries of central and eastern Europe. It allows employees of foreign companies to work in Germany as contract workers who provide services to German companies. The foreign company acts as subcontractor to a German firm, and the workers remain under contract to their foreign employer. The duration is limited to 2-3 years. The foreign firm must ensure the exit of the workers but the local German company also bears some responsibility for enforcement. Part of the contract payment is withheld until the workers return home. Bilateral contract worker agreements include country-specific quotas that can be adapted to the German labour market situation.

Source: IOM, OECD.

Key questions
o   What kinds of workers tend to be covered by bilateral labour agreements? Do countries prefer to take a bilateral approach to lower skilled labour?
o   What has been the experience with bilateral agreements? What implementation challenges have been encountered?
o   What are the strengths and weaknesses of such agreements? Are they likely to increase in the future?
o   What lessons can we learn from these agreements in terms of the negotiations on GATS mode 4?

Regional schemes

Regional trade agreements (RTAs) approach labour mobility in a wide variety of ways. Some agreements cover mobility of people in general, including permanent migration and non-workers; others offer free movement of labour, including entry to the local labour market; some are limited to facilitating movement for certain kinds of trade- or investment-related activities; and still others are, like the GATS, confined to temporary movement and only for service suppliers (and explicitly exclude entry to the labour market or permanent migration). While some agreements cover workers at all skill levels, most are limited to more highly skilled workers.

These different approaches reflect a range of factors, including the geographic proximity of the parties, their similarities in levels of development, and cultural and historical ties. Generally, agreements among countries enjoying geographic proximity and similar levels of development have a more liberal approach to labour mobility than agreements between geographically distant countries of differing levels of development, but this is not always the case.

An important factor in labour mobility is the extent to which countries are aiming at deep integration agreements or at agreements more concerned with opening or facilitating trade. The former tend to result in agreements with free labour mobility (or close to it), while the latter focus on provision of certain forms of mobility for certain categories of persons related to trade. Within each of these forms, the agreements generally contain some similar basic provisions, with differences reflecting the depth and extent of access granted, rather than a fundamentally different approach. Agreements often use each other, and the GATS, as a model for key provisions (*e.g.* related to exceptions).

A few other general observations can be made about labour mobility in RTAs:

- Although some agreements (*e.g.* the EU and, for the highly skilled, CARICOM) allow general mobility of people and/or confer immigration rights, the majority provide only special access or facilitation of access under existing immigration arrangements.[14] In most agreements, labour mobility does not override general migration legislation, and parties retain broad discretion to grant, refuse and administer residence permits and visas.

- Right of labour mobility does not automatically entail the right to practice a certain profession; national regulations for licensing and recognition of qualifications still apply, and candidates must meet all criteria and conditions. In addition, specific professions or service sectors must be open to foreign suppliers. Many agreements exclude certain service sectors from coverage or apply special rules to certain sectors.

- Some agreements no longer deal with mobility under the trade in services section, but group intra-corporate transferees, service suppliers and investors together in a separate chapter on movement of natural persons more generally. While still focused on trade-related movement, they are no longer limited simply to trade in services, but can include investors and business people from other sectors (*e.g.* manufacturing).

Box 1.3 presents examples of different approaches to regional labour mobility. While comparison is difficult, the agreements can be said, broadly speaking, to range from reasonably ambitious schemes covering general freedom of movement for the highly skilled (CARICOM), to agreements that provide for access for certain groups (NAFTA), to a system that does not provide access *per se*, but facilitates the mobility of certain groups by minimising the migration procedures attached to their movement (APEC).

---

14. Of course, the EU agreement is not at all representative. While normally included in all OECD work on RTAs, the EU is actually a deep integration agreement, an economic and monetary union where the free circulation of people across member states' borders is one of founding principles and one of the four fundamental freedoms upon which the union is based. In this case, therefore, member states' migration legislation is required to assist the overriding economic objective of eliminating all barriers to the EU-wide movement of people, capital, services and goods.

Box 1.3. Three approaches to regional labour mobility

The type of mobility envisaged under the Caribbean Community (CARICOM[15]) is towards the most open end of the continuum. CARICOM provides for the free movement of university graduates, other professionals and skilled persons, and selected occupations,[16] as well as freedom of travel and exercise of a profession. It eliminates passport requirements, facilitates entry at immigration points, and eliminates work permit requirements for CARICOM nationals. Foreigners generally receive equivalent treatment to nationals (subject to certain reservations made by each country). Exceptions cover activities involving the exercise of governmental authority and measures to protect public morals, human, animal and plant life, and national security; maintain public order and safety; and secure compliance with the laws of a member state (these basically reflect the exceptions found in the GATS).

The North American Free Trade Agreement (NAFTA[17]) is more limited and focuses on facilitating the movement of business people. The agreement is limited to temporary entry, defined negatively as being "without the intent to establish permanent residence", and applies only to citizens of parties. Access is basically limited to four higher-skill categories: traders and investors, intra-company transferees, business visitors and professionals (detailed definitions are provided). However, these groups are not limited to services and may include persons in activities related to agriculture or manufacturing. Labour certification or labour market assessment/tests are removed for all four groups, Work permits are required for traders and investors, intra-company transferees and professionals, but not business visitors. Although visas are still required, fees for processing applications are limited to the approximate cost of services rendered.

Existing general immigration requirements (*e.g.* related to public health or national security) still apply. Entry can also be refused if it may adversely affect settlement of a labour dispute in progress at the intended place of employment, or the employment of any person who is involved in such a dispute. Dispute settlement provisions cannot be invoked for a refusal to grant temporary entry, unless the matter involves a pattern of practice and the business person has exhausted the available administrative remedies.

---

15. CARICOM: Antigua and Barbuda, the Bahamas, Barbados, Belize, Dominica, Grenada, Guyana, Haiti, Jamaica, St. Kitts and Nevis, St. Lucia, St. Vincent and the Grenadines, Suriname, Trinidad and Tobago. The Bahamas does not participate in the common market and Haiti is not yet a full member.

16. Graduates of universities (several regional universities are named but others also are included), media workers, sports persons, musicians and artists, and workers in the entertainment and tourism industries.

17. NAFTA: Canada, Mexico, the United States.

Box 1.3. Three approaches to regional labour mobility (cont'd.)

The United States provides "Trade NAFTA" (TN) visas for professionals, which are valid for one year and are renewable.[18] Canadians can receive TN status at the port of entry on presentation of a letter from a US employer, but until 1 January, 2004, Mexicans had to arrange for their employer to file a labour condition application and then apply for a visa at the US embassy in Mexico. Similarly, until that date, the United States applied an annual quota of 5 500 Mexican professionals

The Asia Pacific Economic Co-operation (APEC[19]) Forum does not contain any specific market access arrangements related to labour mobility; periods of, and conditions for, temporary entry vary. APEC arrangements exclude the self-employed and unskilled or semiskilled labour and focus on business mobility, and in particular information exchange; dialogue with business; development and implementation of immigration standards; and capacity building to help streamline temporary entry, stay and departure processing for business people. In-principle agreements have been reached to improve application processing times for temporary entry permits for executives and senior managers on intra-corporate transfers and for specialists.

Although APEC does not grant any right of entry, it has established a scheme to facilitate the entry of business visitors under the APEC Business Travel Card Scheme. The card is valid for three years and provides multiple short-term business entries, with stays of two or three months on each arrival. Cardholders are required to present their passports, but receive expedited airport processing and are not required to submit separate applications for business visitor visas.[20] Participating economies commit to implement the scheme on a best endeavours basis and are free to maintain existing visa requirements for business visitors.[21] All economies retain the right to refuse an individual without providing reasons or to refuse entry to APEC Business Travel Card holders at the border.

---

18. Criteria include: the profession is on the NAFTA list; the candidate meets the specific criteria for that profession; and is licensed in the state of destination to practice his/her profession; the prospective position requires someone in that capacity; and the candidate is going to work for a US employer.

19. APEC: Australia; Brunei Darussalam; Canada; Chile; China; Hong Kong, China; Indonesia; Japan; Korea; Malaysia; Mexico; New Zealand; Papua New Guinea; Peru; Philippines; Russia; Singapore; Chinese Taipei; Thailand; United States; Vietnam.

20. There is no limit on the number of cards, and almost 4 000 have been issued to date. Fees vary among the participating economies. The scheme is open to citizens of participating APEC economies who are *bona fide* business people. It does not include spouses and children; persons who wish to engage in paid employment or working holidays; professional athletes, news correspondents, entertainers, musicians, artists, and persons engaged in similar occupations.

21. Currently 14 APEC economies are participating in the scheme: Australia; Brunei Darussalam; Chile; China; Hong Kong, China; Indonesia; Japan; Korea; Malaysia; New Zealand; Peru; the Philippines; Chinese Taipei; and Thailand. While more countries are expected to join in the near future, neither the United States nor Canada are planning to participate.

Key questions

o   What are the different levels of ambition in regional initiatives to promote labour mobility? What are the factors influencing the perception of what is feasible within a given regional arrangement?

o   What categories of persons are covered by these schemes? Business persons? Professionals? A wider range of temporary workers, including more than service suppliers? Are these schemes broader than those for service suppliers (*i.e.* broader than GATS mode 4)?

o   What has been the experience with regional schemes to promote labour mobility?

o   What have been their strengths and weaknesses?

o   What sorts of implementation challenges have been encountered?

o   To what extent have the schemes actually been used and promoted increased mobility?

o   What impact has regional labour mobility had on local labour markets? Is there a gender bias in the provisions or in their application? A skill level bias?

References

IOM (2002), *Diaspora Support to Migration and Development: Challenges and Potentials*, Vol. 4, IOM Series International Dialogue on Migration, IOM, Geneva.

Lowell, L. (2001), "Policy Responses to the International Mobility of Skilled Labour", ILO, Geneva.

Nielson, J. (2003), "Labor Mobility in Regional Trade Agreements" in Aaditya Mattoo and Antonia Carzaniga (eds.), *Moving People to Deliver Services*, World Bank/Oxford University Press, Washington, DC.

OECD (2000), *Globalisation, Migration and Development*, OECD, Paris.

OECD (2001), "Service Providers on the Move: A Closer Look at Labour Mobility and the GATS" TD/TC/WP(2001)26/FINAL, available at www.oecd.org.

OECD (2002), "Labour Shortages and the Need for Immigrants", in *International Mobility of the Highly Skilled,* OECD, Paris.

OECD (2003), *Employment Outlook*, OECD, Paris.

OECD (2004), *Proceedings of the Montreux Seminar on the Bilateral Agreements and Other Forms of Recruitment of Labour, OECD, Paris.*

OECD/SOPEMI (1998), "Report on the Temporary Employment of Foreigners in Several OECD Countries", in *Trends in International Migration*, OECD, Paris.

OECD/SOPEMI (2000), *Trends in International Migration*, OECD, Paris.

Ruhs, M. (2003), "Temporary Foreign Worker Programmes: Policies, Adverse Consequences, and the Need to Make Them Work", ILO Working Papers, Perspectives on Labour Migration, Geneva.

Sexton, J.J. (2003), "A Review of Relevant Labour Market Measures in Ireland", paper prepared for the *Seminar on Bilateral Labour Agreements and Other Forms of Recruitment of Foreign Workers*, organised jointly by the OECD (DELSA) and the Swiss Federal Office of Immigration, Integration and Emigration, Montreux 19-20 June.

Winters, A., T. Walmsley, K.W. Zhen and R. Grynberg (2003), *Liberalising Temporary Movement of Natural Persons: An Agenda for the Development Round*, Blackwell Publishing, Oxford.

Chapter 2

Managing the Impact of Temporary Foreign Workers on Countries of Origin and Destination

This chapter reviews key issues with respect to managing the impact of foreign workers on countries of origin and destination. Freer movement of foreign service providers can lead to concerns about a potentially negative impact on the level of employment and wages of nationals in receiving countries. There is also a range of specific migration issues, such as managing overstaying, promoting brain circulation over brain drain and maximising the benefits of remittances. These objectives can only be fully achieved in co-operation between sending and receiving countries and when migrants maintain links with their countries of origin.

Introduction

In terms of managing the impact of temporary foreign workers, three basic points should be noted.

First, there are big differences among various types of temporary foreign workers. Among those covered by GATS mode 4, issues and impacts will vary. While relatively few concerns may be raised about business visitors and intra-corporate transferees, contractual service suppliers who are employees of foreign firms or who are independent professionals tend to raise more questions. Foreign employees of domestic firms are also the subject of many concerns.[22]

Second, temporary foreign workers tend to be concentrated in certain (mainly high- and semi-skilled service) sectors – health, education (particularly higher education), information technology, hospitality and catering,

---

22. Not all WTO members see foreign employees of domestic firms as being covered by GATS mode 4 (see Annex A).

construction and agriculture – but the issues raised vary among these sectors (World Bank, 2003).

Third, it should be recalled that the phenomenon of temporary foreign workers takes place in a context of difficult and varied challenges for migration authorities. These include managing migration of family members of migrants, asylum seekers and refugees, as well as dealing with the growing phenomenon of people smuggling and other forms of clandestine migration (OECD, 2002a). These challenges form an important backdrop for discussions of trade and migration.

Concerns in receiving countries: labour market, social and security issues

In receiving countries, freer movement of foreign service providers can lead to concerns about the potentially negative impact on the level of employment and wages of their nationals. (A further concern, that temporary entry will lead to permanent migration, is discussed below). While much attention focuses on flows from developing to developed countries, labour migration and mode 4 movement are in fact a wider phenomenon. Migration between developed countries is significant, and a number of developing countries are receivers of labour from other developing countries.

Wages and social security

The GATS provides considerable flexibility for countries to address concerns relating to the impact on the employment of nationals, a flexibility WTO members have freely exercised. The commitments of 50 WTO members provide for the application of domestic minimum wage laws, often coupled with other laws regarding conditions and hours of work and social security. Also, 22 WTO members have reserved the right to suspend commitments in the event of disputes between labour and management. Bilateral labour agreements likewise contain provisions on wages and working conditions.

Many countries insist on parity of wages and conditions for foreign and national workers.[23] Unions argue that wage parity is necessary to preserve hard-won working conditions and wage levels (Waghorne, 2003). There are also concerns about the exploitation of foreign workers; once foreign workers are in a country with a higher cost of living, they have the same wage needs as everyone else and their country of origin is irrelevant. However, some

---

23. The rules for EU member countries, for instance, are very strict and require foreign residents to be paid the same salary and to be granted the same level of social protection as nationals.

developing countries argue that insistence on wage parity undermines their comparative advantage and that, from an economic point of view, wage gaps can be justified in some cases by differing levels of productivity, skills and education. Others argue that wage parity *per se* is less a problem than the costly administrative hurdle of employers having to demonstrate wage parity before hiring foreign workers (Chanda, 1999).

There are questions, also, about the extent to which wage requirements are enforced. It is difficult to control wage levels for foreign workers, and there are abuses and even cases of modern slavery. There is also emerging controversy about companies with foreign subsidiaries importing workers from their home countries as intra-corporate transferees or contract service suppliers (who may not be subject to wage parity and other requirements; see below).

The wage gap between the home and host country may also be such that the worker may be prepared to work for less than the average salary of national workers (Werner, 1996). Further, when the worker's stay in the host country is conditional upon having a job, or is tied to a specific employer, she/he may be in a position of weakness *vis-à-vis* the employer.

Even where wage parity laws are enforced, some argue that foreign workers create a competitive challenge because of differences in social security systems and contributions. Where work is subcontracted to a foreign company (*e.g.* in the construction sector in Germany), social security contributions for project workers are often paid through the foreign company according to the provisions in the foreign company's home country (Winters *et al.*, 2003). Some argue that this creates a competitive advantage for companies that hire temporary foreign workers, for whom social security contributions may be lower.

While exempting foreign workers from national social security contributions raises competitiveness concerns, it is also inequitable to require foreign workers to contribute to social security programmes from which they receive no, or minimal, benefits. One proposed solution is to pay social security charges from temporary foreign workers into separate funds and distribute them to the family/community of the worker or reimburse the worker upon return to his/her home country. Another idea (Winters *et al.*, 2003) is to separate short-term social programmes (*e.g.* health insurance cover for the duration of stay) from longer-term protection which temporary foreign workers do not need and for which they will not qualify (*e.g.* pensions). Workers would contribute to short-term programmes but, for the long-term programmes, either their contributions would be refunded or they would contribute at the rates of their country of origin. However, this does not resolve the competitiveness issue.

Do foreign workers displace nationals? Do they drive down wages?

It is also argued that temporary foreign workers lower wages and working conditions and displace nationals working in the same industry. The issue of complementarities and substitution between foreign and domestic workers is a very complex one with nuances and differences according to activities, regions and nationalities (see Coppel *et al.,* 2001, for a full review[24]). Some arguments are recalled here as an aid to reflection.

Some argue that temporary foreign workers are generally more a supplement to, than a substitute for, local labour. They are often brought in to fill a labour need, either relative (*e.g.* reflecting the economic cycle) or absolute (*e.g.* lack of qualified personnel) and do not necessarily exert downward pressure on wages. It is also argued that it may simply not be profitable for companies to hire only temporary foreign workers instead of permanent staff as training is an additional activity and expense for the firm. While temporary workers may make it possible to respond very flexibly to market needs, employers may have limited interest in letting experienced people go, only to have to train new recruits and incur learning-curve costs (Werner, 1996). In the case of mobility of the highly skilled, firms insist that when they look for temporary foreign service providers, they do so not primarily for reasons of cost (lower wages), but in order to find the most qualified person to perform a task (OECD, 2002a).

However, others argue that the availability of temporary foreign workers undermines pressures to address labour shortages through increased training of nationals or improvement in pay and working conditions. For example, some have argued that temporary employment of foreign nurses undermines efforts to improve conditions and wages for nurses, *i.e.* it prevents developed country governments from having to address the root cause of their nursing shortages. Companies applying to bring in temporary foreign workers can be required to demonstrate their commitment to the training and employment of nationals (*e.g.* in the Australian scheme).

Some have also questioned whether the availability of temporary foreign workers as contractual service suppliers creates an incentive for companies to seek savings by outsourcing particular activities within the domestic market. This may include outsourcing locally to foreign established companies that may bring in workers as intra-corporate transferees (*i.e.* potentially not subject to strict labour market tests or wage parity requirements). This has been argued

---

24. Issues include, for example, whether new waves of temporary foreign workers compete with persons from former waves of migration, the degree of competition among unqualified workers and the extent of competition among all three of these categories in a context of high unemployment.

to result in job losses in national firms. (The rise in offshore outsourcing, an easier and cheaper solution for some firms given employment and security-related visa restrictions on temporary foreign workers, is also becoming increasingly controversial in terms of the impact on employment of nationals).

Others acknowledge that the adjustment stresses that mode 4 liberalisation may engender can be both large and concentrated on vulnerable sections of society (Winters *et al.*, 2003). Chaudhuri *et al.* (2003) note that the timing and extent of liberalisation may need to be managed to ensure that existing compensatory schemes can cope. They suggest that, in the longer term, more active redistribution will be required to try to ensure that fewer nationals of developed countries are in sectors where they compete with foreign workers. They see this as involving education and training, as well as possible asset distribution. However, they argue that the challenges for mode 4 liberalisation are neither more nor less serious than those created for less skilled workers by imports of labour-intensive goods from developing countries, a problem managed by policies to ease adjustment among local less skilled workers in developed countries. However, movement of less skilled workers between developing countries may create challenges for countries with more limited capacity to fund and implement adjustment policies for displaced locals.

Are social adjustment costs better or worse for temporary workers?

Some argue that social adjustment costs are worse for temporary workers as they have no incentive to fit into the host country. The long-term risks of extensive reliance on temporary workers from abroad are the creation of ghettoes of foreign workers with no strong attachment to the host country and no incentive to contribute to local community life. Temporary movement also entails "turnover" costs, both for employing firms and society (*e.g.* in terms of recurring investment in firm-specific technical training and limited social integration). However, others argue that temporary movement can avert some of the social and political costs of permanent migration. Assimilation problems are less likely with temporary migration and illegal immigration can also be reduced by the availability of an orderly process for allowing legitimate temporary workers to come and go on a predictable basis. Some argue that movement under mode 4 can be a partial substitute for permanent migration (Ghosh, 1998); if temporary movement is made easier and more predictable, it may be preferable to permanent migration for the migrant.

Security considerations

Any attempt to facilitate mobility must confront today's increased concerns about national security. Liberalised movement requires security clearance to be quick and reliable.[25] The challenge politically is to separate security arguments from labour market or service export considerations. As Winters *et al.* (2001) note, even national security has a finite price in terms of civil liberties and economic well-being. Economic efficiency does not require one to neglect security considerations, but it does require that if there are tradeoffs between security and income, they are balanced.

Key questions

o What are the market benefits for destination countries?

o How important is wage parity? What kinds of equitable solutions can be found regarding social security contributions?

o What is the impact of foreign workers on nationals? What kinds of tools can be used to manage these impacts?

o Are adjustment costs less for temporary foreign workers than for other types of migration? What measures can be taken to facilitate integration and quality of life for temporary migrant workers while in a foreign country? Do these measures vary for various groups (*i.e.* between high- and low- skill occupations)?

o How big a challenge is the new security context for facilitating movement?

Issues in countries of origin: remittances, brain circulation and broader trade linkages

Although the impact of brain drain on some countries is undeniable, labour migration can also have positive repercussions for countries of origin, in particular through remittances (see below), but also through migrants' acquisition of social and business networks, enhanced skills and financial resources. The potential benefits of migration for countries of origin are enhanced when migrants return (temporary or circular migration) or maintain links with their countries of origin.

---

25. In the United States, the National Academy of Sciences warned that critical research had been impeded by visa restrictions that had blocked or delayed the entry of foreign scientists. Theatre and music companies also claim to have repeatedly been forced to cancel or change performances because many foreign-born artists can no longer get visas (*Financial Times*, 29 January 2003).

Brain drain

Brain drain, or the emigration of highly skilled workers leading to skill shortages, reductions in output and tax shortfalls, is of significant concern to countries of origin. Brain drain can reinforce the development trap when communities of skilled persons in developed countries attract other skilled persons and further deplete weaker communities in developing countries. Costs can also be substantial in terms of the country of origin's investment in training and education; higher education is heavily subsidised in many developing countries and skilled migrants carry away scarce human capital built with public investment (World Bank, 2003). This is particularly troubling in sectors such as healthcare which have a direct impact on the ability of developing nations to maintain and improve the quality of life of their citizens and to achieve equitable development and integration into the global economy (OECD, 2004).

Workers seeking to move under mode 4 are often the most industrious and best qualified, and their departure may have a greater negative impact on the sending country's economy than that of less highly skilled workers (WTO, 1998). Mode 4 can thus exacerbate fears of a brain drain. However, the key point is also that mode 4 is only *temporary* migration, and temporary movement can partially mitigate some of the negative consequences of labour migration.

Indeed, the costs of temporary movement of skilled people can be offset by the benefits to their home country when they return with enhanced skills and contacts in the international business community (*e.g.* Indian returnees from Silicon Valley have been the main force behind the growth of the Indian software industry). The current trend towards temporary migration has seen a growing rate of return among highly qualified workers.[26] (However, if returns are to take place, economic and political conditions in the home country have to be favourable; see below). This "brain circulation" can allow the short-term costs of temporary movement of skilled people to be balanced by later benefits to their home country.

However, where need is great and skills are scarce, even the temporary loss of skilled persons can be a problem. The health sector is a prominent example, and in particular nursing shortages in a number of developing countries that face public health crises. In such cases, complementary policies may be necessary. One such initiative is the Commonwealth Code of Practice for the

---

26. A survey of 1 500 Chinese and Indians working in Silicon Valley found that 50% go back at least once a year and 5% visit at least five times. In addition, 74% of Indian respondents and 53% of Chinese intended to start a business in their home country (UNCTAD, 2003).

International Recruitment of Health Workers, which provides guidelines that take into account the potential impact of such recruitment in the sending country. The Code is intended to discourage targeted recruitment of health workers from countries that are themselves experiencing shortages. Active recruitment policies can of course be differentiated from allowing the entry of self-selected migrants; in other words, while recognising the right of people to choose where they want to live and the conditions under which they work, it is important to devise a policy which prevents practices that can undermine progress in development.

"Brain waste" is an issue faced by temporary skilled workers who are unable to use their skills and training. Recognition of their skills and qualifications would allow them more opportunities and would provide gains for both sending and receiving countries.

Finally, labour migration and mode 4 movement are not limited to flows from developing to developed countries. Migration between developed countries is also significant, and brain drain is an issue of concern to some developed countries, such as Australia and Canada. A number of developing countries are also receivers of labour from other developing countries.

Remittances

Remittances, defined as the portion of an international migrant's earnings sent back from a host country to his/her country of origin, have become a key source of global finance and one of the greatest potential benefits for countries of origin of temporary workers. The total value of remittances transferred through official channels worldwide more than doubled between 1988 and 1999, with officially recorded workers' remittances amounting to USD 72.3 billion in 2001 (World Bank, 2003). The total amount may be higher, however, since many go through informal channels. In low-income countries, remittances are on average about 1.9% of GDP and can be as much as 26.5% (Lesotho). In most developing countries, remittances are a larger source of income than official development assistance (ODA) and in low-income countries they are also two to three times larger than total foreign direct investment (FDI) (Ratha, 2003). Indeed, the pattern of remittances is much more evenly spread among developing countries than FDI. Remittances are also generally less volatile than other financial flows and are generally unaffected by international financial crises.

Many remittances are sent directly to individuals and households; in some cases they amount to over 50% of total household incomes. While this makes them important for reducing individual/household poverty, remittances also have enormous potential for increasing local and national economic growth in countries of origin if directed towards longer-term investment strategies.

However, to date, the transformation of migrant remittances into productive investments has been hampered by inadequate economic structures and insufficient institutional and policy frameworks (Ratha, 2003).

Barriers to official transfers of funds are currently the greatest obstacle to maximising the benefits of remittances. Transfers via official bank channels are often complicated and lengthy and are often inaccessible for migrants who are unable to open bank accounts in their countries of residence owing to their temporary situation or status. Frequently, the only alternatives are private companies, which generally charge high fees. Currently, the average cost of an official transfer is about 13%, and can often exceed 20%, of the total amount (Ratha, 2003). As a result, an unknown amount of money passes through informal channels, where it is subject to risks such as fraud and theft. It is essential to reduce the cost of remittance transfers, particularly through the establishment of efficient banking systems in countries of origin and increased access by migrants to legitimate transfer avenues, if the benefits of remittances are to be fully maximised (see Box 2.1).

Box 2.1. Managing remittances: some initiatives from Mexico

Under Mexico's "3 for 1" joint investment programme, migrant associations are encouraged to invest in community projects by matching each dollar spent by migrant associations with an additional dollar each from the municipal, provincial and federal governments.

Mexico has also attempted to address the difficulty of opening bank accounts in migrants' country of residence. The *matricula consular* identity cards, issued to Mexican citizens living in the United States legally or illegally, are increasingly accepted as proof of identity when opening accounts at US banks. This allows migrants to use banks to transfer funds cheaply and transparently, rather than having to rely on private companies that charge exorbitant fees.

US banks increasingly sense the business opportunity represented by these new clients. Some have responded by introducing schemes such as dual automatic teller machine (ATM) cards, which allow a party in the United States to deposit funds that can be withdrawn by a recipient abroad as an alternative to more expensive wire transfers. To overcome immigrants' mistrust of financial institutions, some banks have also linked up with churches or other community organisations serving immigrants and provide Spanish-speaking staff. Traditional providers of wire transfers (such as Western Union which dominates the USD 122 billion international wire market) are halving the costs of transferring money.

Sources: Mexico's contribution to the Diaspora Support to Migration and Development Workshop, IOM 84th Council Session, December 2002; Ratha (2003); "Banking for Immigrants: Reaching Out", *The Economist*, 22 February 2003; "Money from US Sustains Mexico", *International Herald Tribune*, 29 October 2003.

Finally, remittances are sent by a much wider group than mode 4, including permanent emigrants and persons working outside of the service sector. Gains in remittances should not therefore simply be equated with gains from mode 4. Indeed, to the extent that mode 4 movement is, to date, largely limited to higher skilled workers, there is some evidence to suggest that better educated emigrants are less likely to send remittances and are also likely to remit a smaller share of their incomes (IOM, 2003a). This could equally be an argument for extension of mode 4 commitments to cover lower-skilled workers who are the largest source of remittance flows.

Links between mode 4 and other types of trade

There are clear links between the temporary movement of service suppliers and the promotion of FDI. The overseas networks and exposure resulting from movement of service providers may induce FDI in the country of origin of migrants. Moreover, establishment of commercial presence in a country can create possibilities for that country to export various services through outsourcing and electronic delivery to the country that is the source of the investment or even third countries.

Returning migrants and diaspora are also an important source of FDI. Chanda (2003) notes that governments can induce return migration and maximise the use of the experience, skills, networks and financial capital of return migrants by introducing policies to streamline investment procedures for interested returnees, involve return migrants more actively in policy making, and encourage return migrants to contribute to and network with public sector institutions so that their contributions are not confined to the private sector. Steps can also be taken to encourage the participation of the diaspora in the domestic economy, in recognition of the fact that much of the spillover from mode 4 arises from diaspora-related financial and other contributions to the economy. For instance, governments could set up special investment procedures and incentives to attract diaspora investment, set up systems to track the diaspora and to institutionalise and develop the diaspora network for investment, research and training, securing projects and contracts, and for collaborative ventures.

Temporary foreign workers have also contributed to growth in trade via outsourcing to the home country. Chanda (2003) notes that the presence of temporary Indian workers in the United States has had much to do with raising the awareness of US companies about the pool of skilled labour within India. Experience working with Indians in their home country may also have contributed to companies' decision to outsource work to India. Also, by generating opportunities for employment, training and skills in migrants' country of origin, outsourcing can help to ensure the temporary nature of mode 4 movement, creating economic and institutional growth that provides incentives for workers to return after periods abroad.

Promoting labour exports

Countries of origin hoping to maximise the benefits of supply of services through temporary labour migration must ensure that the skills of their temporary labour migrants match the needs of the labour market in receiving countries. Many countries have used bilateral labour agreements with countries of destination to ensure compatibility between workers' skills and demand and to gain privileged access to labour markets in key sectors of demand, such as health.

Chanda (2003) notes that governments need to ensure standards and quality in order to promote exports. They need to invest appropriately in education and training and in upgrading the relevant infrastructure. Competitive domestic markets can also contribute to raising standards, as can the development of standards for licensing and accreditation of temporary foreign workers (and mechanisms for their enforcement). Moreover, governments and professional bodies should benchmark to international standards, including to facilitate the negotiation of mutual recognition agreements with key trading partners.

Other studies underline that, if the aim is to institutionalise temporary labour migration or labour exports as a component of national development, sending countries also need to work to ensure the protection of the rights of their temporary migrant workers in the receiving countries (as well as channels for the regularisation of remittances). Indeed, some middle-income countries have also been developing migration management structures that encourage and support their migrants throughout the entire migration process. The Philippines, which currently deploys about 900 000 migrant workers annually to over 165 countries, has adopted a progressive legal framework and well-integrated government machinery to manage the sending of Filipinos abroad. The government has initiated several programmes for the protection and promotion of overseas workers, including regulation of recruitment, verification of employment documents, provision of pre-employment orientation and provision of protection abroad through embassies and missions (IOM, 2002a; 2003b).

Key questions

o What safeguards can be put in place to limit the possibility of a skills shortage caused by temporary movement in countries of origin?

o How can mode 4 contribute to the benefits of "brain circulation" for countries of origin?

o How can countries of origin best manage remittance flows? Is there evidence that remittances are higher from temporary migrants than from those who leave permanently? Is there a difference in remittance patterns between high-skilled and low-skilled migrants?

o How can countries of origin use mode 4 to enhance other forms of trade?

o How can domestic policies contribute to the use of temporary labour migration or labour exports for development?

o What can countries of origin do to ensure the protection of their citizens abroad?

Ensuring temporariness: overstaying and return incentives

The prospect that greater temporary movement will lead to permanent migration can be a concern for both countries of origin and countries of destination. Some countries of origin fear the permanent loss of sometimes scarce skilled workers, while some destination countries can fear loss of control over migration.

It is certainly a reality that temporary movement can be a first step to permanent residence, but it is not a simple one. First, in some countries (*e.g.* Australia, United Kingdom, Switzerland and the United States), certain categories of temporary workers are permitted to change visa categories and thus apply to stay. In this way, temporary entry can be used to pre-select candidates for permanent migration. Other countries maintain a clear distinction between visa schemes for temporary workers and those allowing application for permanent residence. Second, overstaying is a risk with all forms of temporary movement, including tourists and students. It can be argued that regular schemes for the temporary movement of workers can help discourage employers from employing those who lack permission to work by making temporary workers legally available for seasonal activities.

Evidence varies on the extent to which temporary movement becomes permanent. It is estimated that about half of those admitted under the US temporary highly skilled worker programme ultimately remain in the country as permanent residents (Lowell, 2001). However, only a relatively small proportion of holders of UK work permits seem to settle permanently; in 1998, 3 160 work permit holders became permanent residents, while approximately 70 000-80 000 work permits are approved each year (UK Home Office, 2001). Other studies of temporary worker programmes (Ruhs, 2003) indicate that temporary worker programmes tend to become longer in duration and larger in size than initially envisaged.

The factors involved in return migration, and the policies adopted to encourage return, vary considerably from country to country. They also vary depending on the type of temporary migration involved (*e.g.* seasonal workers vs. intra-corporate transferees, etc.). There are few data available to evaluate the many potential factors that may contribute to return migration. Broadly speaking, there are two main approaches: sanctions and incentives.

Sanctions

Most temporary worker schemes involve some sanction mechanism for ensuring that entrants do not overstay. These include:

- Withholding part of the pay of contractual service suppliers until they (or, in the case of a firm, their workers) leave the country.

- Requiring firms or individuals to place a bond which is forfeited in the case of non-departure (Hatcher, 2003).

- Fining the domestic sponsoring company for workers who do not leave and withdrawing their right to sponsor future workers.

Many of these mechanisms are more easily applied to firms than to individuals. Indeed, the fact that there are fewer enforcement difficulties for intra-corporate transferees – where the local company can be penalised – than for independent service providers accounts in part for the more liberal treatment accorded to the former. However, Ruhs (2003) suggests that employer sanctions have often proved relatively ineffective; even where penalties have been severe, there is evidence that illegal employment of foreign workers has continued to increase.

Incentives

In addition to sanctions, incentive mechanisms can be used both by the country of destination and the country of origin. Experience with bilateral labour agreements suggests that prospects of re-employment in following years can act as an incentive for migrants to return home. For example, in an agreement between Spain and Ecuador, workers must present their passports with the original visa at the Spanish Consulate in Ecuador within a month of return to be eligible to be recruited again.[27] The possibility for employers to rehire the same workers the following year also discourages them from permitting illegal overstaying (*e.g.* the Canadian Commonwealth Caribbean and Mexican Seasonal Agricultural Worker Programme).

---

27. Agreement between Spain and the Republic of Ecuador on the Regulation of Migratory Flows.

Other incentives are operated by the governments of countries of origin and are largely aimed at encouraging the return of highly qualified nationals. As part of their effort to promote human capital development, countries such as Colombia, Ghana, Guyana, India, Iran, Iraq, Pakistan, Peru, the Philippines, Korea, Sri Lanka and Turkey have launched various initiatives to encourage the return of qualified personnel from abroad. These initiatives may take the form of specific incentives (*e.g.* tax exemptions, financial assistance with removal costs or business seed capital, citizenship rights for spouses and children), or of attractive opportunities in the home country. Chinese Taipei,[28] Korea and Singapore have all fostered return migration by encouraging domestic investment in R&D (World Bank, 2003).

Provision of reintegration assistance to returnees is another measure adopted by some countries to facilitate return. Such assistance may be vital to ensuring that returns are sustainable. A recent IOM study in Bangladesh (IOM, 2002b) found that relatively little reintegration assistance was available to temporary workers returning home from the Gulf states. The authors argue that the process of reintegration should begin well before the actual return of the temporary migrant worker and that greater effort should be made by countries of origin to use the specialised skills acquired by temporary migrant workers while working abroad.

Key questions

o What are the challenges faced by migration authorities in preventing overstaying?

o How can countries of origin and destination co-operate better to prevent overstaying by temporary workers?

o How effective are different types of incentives, including reintegration packages, used to encourage the return of temporary workers?

o What lessons can be learned from government attempts to impose sanctions on either employers or migrants when overstaying occurs?

o What kinds of measures have been successful in promoting return migration?

o Should the role of government be simply the facilitation and removal of obstacles to return or should it be to take steps to actively promote return?

Policy co-ordination

To increase the benefits of temporary foreign labour and mode 4 movement for countries of origin and of destination, as well as for migrants

---

28. Chinese Taipei is reported to have lured back 50 000 scientists who had left the country over the past two decades by expanding the scope of its graduate science programmes and emphasising the country's growing high-technology industry (*International Herald Tribune*, 3 April 2001).

themselves, communication and co-operation between policy makers is essential on two different levels:

- Bilaterally and multilaterally between countries of origin and countries of destination.

- Internally within government agencies between trade, labour market and migration officials.

International co-ordination

International labour migration, by definition, has transnational implications and cannot be managed unilaterally. Bilateral and multilateral policies and dialogue between countries of origin and of destination are the best means of avoiding uncoordinated and uncontrolled movement while maximising the benefits of labour migration for all parties. In particular, co-operation between countries of origin and of destination is necessary to ensure that the skills of temporary foreign workers match the market needs and skills shortages of countries of destination. An example of such policy co-ordination at the bilateral level is the pilot mechanism for the management of regular migration between Italy and Albania, set up with IOM assistance in March 2000, which involved the selection of 5 000 Albanian workers whose professional qualifications fulfilled Italian labour market needs.

Internal co-ordination

While international policy co-ordination is important, work towards a more systemic approach to migration management begins at the national level. Without co-ordination and whole-of-government approaches within countries, progress at an international level is difficult. The increasing trend towards temporary foreign labour programmes, reinforced by the GATS mode 4 negotiations, has implications for trade, migration and labour market officials. Communication and dialogue between these government agencies in the formulation of national policies will greatly enhance the effectiveness and benefits of temporary labour migration programmes.

Key questions
o   How can international co-operation on temporary migration issues be increased?
o   How can policy co-ordination between trade, labour and migration policy officials be improved at the national level?

References

Chanda, R. (1999), "Movement of Natural Persons and Trade in Services: Liberalising Temporary Movement of Labour under the GATS", Indian Council for Research on International Economic Relations, India, www.icrier.res.in.

Chanda R. (2003), "Linkages between Mode 4 and Other GATS Modes of Supply", available at www.oecd.org/ech/meetings/4sxm

Chaudhuri, S., A. Mattoo and R. Self (2003), "Liberalizing Mode 4: A Possible Approach", available www.oecd.org/ech/meetings/4sxm

Coppel J., J.C. Dumont et I. Visco (2001), "Trends in Immigration and Economic Consequences", OECD, ECO/WPK(2001)10, February.

Ghosh, B. (1998), *Huddled Masses and Uncertain Shores: Insights into Irregular Migration*", Book Series: Refugees and Human Rights : Vol. 2, Kluwer Law International.

Iredale, R. (2003), *Return Migration in the Asia Pacific*, Edward Elgar, Cheltenham.

IOM (2002a), *Diaspora Support to Migration and Development: Challenges and Potentials*, Vol. 4 in IOM Series International Dialogue on Migration, IOM, Geneva.

IOM (2002b), "Synthesis Paper on the Studies of Labour Migration Process in Bangladesh", IOM, Dhaka.

IOM (2003a), *The Migration-Development Nexus*, IOM, Geneva.

IOM (2003b), *Labour Migration in Asia: Trends, Challenges, and Policy Responses in Countries of Origin*, IOM, Geneva.

Lowell, L. (2001), "Policy Responses to the International Mobility of Skilled Labour", ILO, Geneva.

Nielson, J. (2003), "Labor Mobility in Regional Trade Agreements", in Aaditya Mattoo and Antonia Carzaniga (eds.), *Moving People to Deliver Services*, World Bank/Oxford University Press, Washington, DC.

OECD (2000), "Globalisation, Migration and Development", TD/TC/WP(2001)26/FINAL, www.oecd.org.

OECD (2001), "Service Providers on the Move: A Closer Look at Labour Mobility and the GATS", TD/TC/WP(2001)26/FINAL, www.oecd.org.

OECD (2002a), "Labour Shortages and the Need for Immigrants", in *International Mobility of the Highly Skilled,* OECD, Paris.

OECD (2002b), *Trends in International Migration*, OECD, Paris.

OECD (2003), *Employment Outlook*, OECD, Paris.

OECD (2004), *Proceedings of the Montreux Seminar on the Bilateral Agreements and Other Forms of Recruitment of Labour,* OECD, Paris.

OECD/SOPEMI (1998), "Report on the Temporary Employment of Foreigners in Several OECD Countries", in *Trends in International Migration*, OECD, Paris.

OECD/SOPEMI (2000), *Trends in International Migration*, OECD, Paris.

PricewaterhouseCoopers (2001), *International Assignments: European Policy and Practice: Key Trends 1999/2000.*

Ratha, D. (2003), "Workers' Remittances: An Important and Stable Source of External Development Finance", in World Bank, *Global Development Finance: Striving for Stability in Development Finance,* Washington, DC.

Ruhs, M. (2003), "Temporary Foreign Worker Programmes: Policies, Adverse Consequences, and the Need to Make Them Work", ILO Working Papers, Perspectives on Labour Migration, Geneva.

UK Home Office (2001), "Migration: An Economic and Social Analysis", Research, Development and Statistics Directorate, Occasional Paper No. 67.

UNCTAD (2003), "Increasing Participation of Developing Countries through liberalization of market access in GATS Mode 4 for Movement of Natural Persons Supplying Services", www.unctad.org

Waghorne, M. (2003), "Mode 4 and Trade Union Concerns", in Aaditya Mattoo and Antonia Carzaniga (eds.), *Moving People to Deliver Services*, World Bank/Oxford University Press, Washington, DC.

Werner, H. (1996), *Temporary Migration for Employment and Training Purposes,* Social Cohesion and Quality of Life, Council of Europe, available at: social.coe.int/en/cohesion/action/ publi/migrants/migrtoc.htm

Winters, A. (2001), "Assessing the Efficiency Gain from Further Liberalisation: A Comment", in P. Sauvé and A. Subramanian (eds.), *Efficiency, Equity and Legitimacy: The Multilateral Trading System and the Millennium*, University of Chicago Press, Chicago.

Winters, A., T. Walmsley, K.W. Zhen and R. Grynberg (2003), *Liberalising Temporary Movement of Natural Persons: An Agenda for the Development Round*, Blackwell Publishing, Oxford.

World Bank (2003), *Global Economic Prospects*, Washington, DC.

WTO (1998), Council for Trade in Services, "Presence of Natural Persons (Mode 4): A Background Note by the Secretariat", S/C/W/75, 8 December.

Chapter 3

Facilitating Access under the GATS

This chapter explores the prospects for progress on mode 4 in the current round of GATS negotiations. In terms of categories of workers, progress might be more difficult for low-skilled labour and foreign employees of domestic companies. Reducing administrative barriers is key for businesses in order to bring in personnel fast enough to meet needs and reduce costs. In this context, the feasibility of a GATS visa is explored. Improving the availability and quality of information is also crucial for business, particularly for small and medium-sized enterprises that often lack the resources to learn about conditions across a range of WTO members.

For what categories of workers can we make progress?

GATS mode 4 is relatively broadly yet poorly defined. In some areas, the GATS provides little guidance (*e.g.* temporary is only defined as excluding permanent); in others, there are differences of view over the scope of coverage (*e.g.* on foreign employees of domestic companies); and matters are further complicated by the fact that members' commitments do not reflect the scope of the agreement (*e.g.* while mode 4 covers service suppliers at all skill levels, commitments have been largely limited to the highly skilled).

The issues that arise for temporary movement, and the degree of political sensitivity, can also vary considerably depending upon the kinds of workers in question and the proposed duration of their stay. Business visitors staying up to 90 days have been relatively uncontroversial in most countries, but other types of entrants have been the focus of greater concern (*e.g.* members of both the House and Senate Judiciary Committees criticised the Office of the US Trade Representative for including provisions allowing the temporary entry of business professionals in the Chile and Singapore free trade agreements, because this was viewed as impinging on Congress' authority over migration matters).

Against this backdrop, it is useful to consider which are the areas in which progress is most likely to be made in the GATS negotiations.

Duration of stay

The GATS mode 4 covers the temporary movement of service suppliers, excluding permanent migration. However, it leaves the definition of temporary to the discretion of individual WTO members (*e.g.* Japan allows foreign business travellers to stay for a maximum of 90 days, and certain categories of intra-corporate transferees for five years). Such flexibility has the advantage of not creating a definitional straightjacket. While there is some degree of convergence among members in terms of the time periods allowed for different categories (*e.g.* most limit business visitors to around three months), there seems little prospect of for achieving more standardisation of duration of stay, and indeed little benefit to be gained. It is perhaps more important to aim at having more WTO members specify, in their schedules, the duration of stay allowed for each category.

The final issue for duration of stay is largely a political one and linked to the type of contract. The longer the permitted presence of the service supplier, the more difficult it is to maintain a distinction between mode 4 and permanent migration, a distinction that provides significant political reassurance. This is also linked to the question of categories of entrants and the perception that some impact the labour market (and hence affect nationals) more directly than others. Indeed, this is clearly reflected in the fact that service suppliers who are intra-corporate transferees tend to benefit from longer durations of stay than individual service suppliers. It is nonetheless important to ensure that duration of stay actually matches the commercial realities of trade in the sector.

Skills level

While there are well-known shortages in some sectors in developed countries (*e.g.* nursing, teaching and information and communication technology), some argue that there will also be a growing shortage of lower-skilled workers in the coming years, as populations age and levels of training and education continue to rise, but demand continues in areas where there is no substitute for human labour (Winters *et al.*, 2003). In spite of this and studies indicating that the greatest global welfare gains come from mobility of lower-skilled labour, few governments have shown an interest to date in including lower-skilled labour in their GATS commitments. GATS commitments are generally limited to business travellers or intra-corporate transferees who are managers, executives or specialists (see Table 3.1).

Table 3.1. Types of natural persons supplying services (horizontal commitments), April 2002

		No. of entries	No. of aggregate entries	% of aggregate entries
Intra-corporate transferees	Executives	56	168	42
	Managers	55		
	Specialists	56		
	Others	1		
Executives		24	110	28
Managers		42		
Specialists		44		
Business visitors	Commercial presence	41	93	23
	Sale negotiations	52		
Contract suppliers		12	12	3
Other		17	17	4
Total[1]		400	400	100

1. Total number of entries by WTO members that have included commitments on mode 4 in the horizontal section of their schedules.

Source: World Trade Organization.

Against this backdrop, is it feasible to look at GATS commitments for lower-skilled workers? A number of developing countries see their main opportunity to participate in the global provision of services as taking place through the movement of unskilled and semiskilled workers.[29] However, as Chaudhuri *et al.* (2003) ask, will venturing too far down the skill ladder undermine the political feasibility of the whole endeavour, given that few countries are today willing to assume multilateral commitments on unskilled labour? They note that choosing a skill threshold that strikes the appropriate balance between economic gains and wider participation on the one hand, and political feasibility on the other, is perhaps the greatest challenge in the current negotiations.

In this regard it is perhaps worth noting that lower-skilled labour is, in many cases, covered under bilateral labour agreements. This might be because the kind of work undertaken by this category of labour is often more regional

---

29. The "Modalities for the Special Treatment for Least Developed Country Members in the Negotiations on Trade in Services" (TN/S/13, 2 September 2003] notes that LDCs have identified mode 4 as important and that members shall, to the extent possible, consider undertaking commitments to provide access, taking into account all categories of natural persons identified by LDCs in their requests.

in character (*i.e.* is it economical to move fruit pickers halfway across the globe, rather than from a neighbouring country?), or there may be close historical ties between the countries. Bilateral labour agreements are often pursued to satisfy demand for labour as well as to diminish migration pressures. Such agreements may offer greater flexibility than GATS commitments.

While there may be limited prospects for including lower-skilled labour in the GATS, questions have also arisen about what to do about groups that may not quite come under the category "highly skilled/managers/executives/specialists", such as junior staff undergoing training as future managers, persons without university qualifications but with useful work experience (*e.g.* in the ICT sector) and persons who may not be highly skilled but who possess essential technical knowledge (technical support personnel).

The category of junior staff undergoing training has been the subject of industry interest, as companies increasingly send employees abroad for training purposes at early stages of their careers before they reach management levels. Because international experience has become more important for promotion, there is pressure to send promising employees who have not yet reached management ranks overseas. Companies also report that ability to offer overseas experience at an early stage is an important factor in competing for the best graduates (graduate training/development accounted for 3.7% of expatriates in a 2001 survey by PricewaterhouseCoopers).[30] The EU has responded to this interest by including "graduate trainees" (persons with a university degree who are transferring for career development or training purposes) in its offer.

In terms of persons with useful work experience, one possibility is to broaden "specialist" or "other persons" to include middle-level personnel. Expanded market access in these categories could be of particular interest to developing countries, although host countries may have concerns about the scope of potentially broader categories and clear definitions would be needed. These might be difficult to achieve in the absence of formal education qualifications.

In terms of technical personnel, some OECD countries currently provide some special treatment for "non-professional essential personnel", *i.e.* personnel with specialised skills but who do not meet the qualification requirements for the highly skilled (*e.g.* aircraft repair and maintenance crews). For example, in Canada, foreign workers who come to oversee the installation

---

30. OECD/SOPEMI (1998) indicates that a number of countries already have a recognised category of trainees, although they tend not to cover intra-corporate transferees (except for senior staff). Most are also subject to quotas under bilateral agreements.

or maintenance of special equipment purchased or leased abroad are not subject to tests to ensure that their employment is beneficial to the Canadian economy and not detrimental to employment opportunities for Canadians. In Germany, workers who install or carry out maintenance repair work or tests on equipment supplied by a foreign enterprise are not required to have work permits provided that they do not remain in Germany for more than three months (OECD, 2001). Given that such personnel may be more relevant for some sectors than others (*e.g.* energy, transport), consideration could be given to sector-specific commitments.

Indeed, sector-specific commitments may be a solution to the question of the appropriate overall skill threshold, particularly in sectors where lower-level qualifications or industry certification might be more important than a university degree (*e.g.* ICT). However, sector-specific commitments may pose challenges for implementation, as few countries have sectoral categories in their immigration laws, and distinguishing between service providers and others has proved difficult. Chaudhuri *et al.* (2003) note that their interviews with immigration authorities suggest that administering sector-specific commitments would be procedurally burdensome and that horizontal commitments applying across all sectors remain easier to administer.

Type of contract?

Most existing GATS commitments relate to intra-corporate transferees or, in some cases, employment-based movement (*e.g.* Australia and the United States). No significant differences exist between the commitments of developed and developing countries in this regard. Countries that acceded to the WTO after 1995 have been more likely to include commitments for "contract suppliers" (*i.e.* employees of a foreign enterprise that has concluded a contract to supply a service in a country but does not have a commercial presence in that market). In some cases, it is specified that these contract suppliers can also be individual (*i.e.* self-employed) service suppliers, not employees of a foreign enterprise (the EC terms this category "independent professionals" in its initial offer).

Chaudhuri *et al.* (2003) look at the three main types of mode 4 movement: employment-based, intra-corporate and contractual service suppliers. They argue that the latter two should be the priority focus for the GATS negotiations.

Employment-based movement

In this case, an individual moves with a prior offer of employment in a host country firm. Examples include the US H1-B visa scheme and the Australian employer-sponsored entry programme. Chaudhuri *et al.* (2003) argue that such movement should not be a priority for the GATS negotiations because:

- Such schemes (in particular H1-B visas) have worked less as a temporary migration scheme than as a selective permanent migration scheme. In practice, employing firms have often performed a screening function, thereby helping to select foreigners for permanent resident status.

- The demand for foreign employees is likely to be determined by domestic economic conditions and, as in the United States, a large number of domestic firms can be relied on to push for increased access.

Others have also argued that it may not be worth prioritising this movement, given that it seems to be less directly a trade matter (Winters *et al.*, 2003). A further point, not raised by the authors, but worth noting, is that not all WTO members see foreign employees of domestic firms as being covered by GATS mode 4 (see Annex A).

Intra-corporate movement

This is already one of the most liberal categories of commitments. Intra-corporate transferees are often permitted longer stays (*e.g.* three years in the United States, EU and Canada, four years in Australia) and are often not subject to economic needs tests (provided the person has been in the prior employment of the firm for a period of at least a year), quotas or wage parity requirements.[31] Chaudhuri *et al.* (2003) see potential for further progress on this category in the current negotiations:

- Where firms have a commercial presence abroad, the intra-corporate route may be a more efficient way of servicing foreign markets than new employment-based movement.

- The emergence of information technology (IT), audiovisual and construction multinationals in countries like India and Brazil suggests that, in addition to the traditionally strong interest of developed country multinationals, some developing countries will also have a strong interest in intra-corporate movement.

- The benefits of this category would be maximised if it were expanded from the current managers, executives and specialists to include a wider

---

31. A look at the actual regimes indicates that the United States imposes neither prevailing wage requirements, nor annual caps on approved petitions for this visa category. Moreover, managers and executives can extend their US stay for up to seven years, while specialists can do so for up to five years.

class of skilled employees, such as those who provide assistance, advice or service to a foreign client, or receive business training, irrespective of their place in the organisational hierarchy.

Contractual service providers

This covers the strictly temporary movement of natural persons to fulfil prior service contracts with host country firms. Chaudhuri *et al.* (2003) suggest that this should be the priority focus for the negotiations because:

- Contract-based movement is more likely to be temporary than employment-based movement. It therefore promises more gains to both home and host countries.

- As temporary movement, contract-based movement is more closely identified with trade in services *per se* than employment-based movement, which can be seen as a direct entry into the labour market (and therefore should be determined by economies' needs for such movement).

- It may also be easier to liberate contract-based movement from economic needs tests (*e.g.* in the EU offer) and wage parity requirements (*e.g.* in the US offer).

- Contract-based movement, like employment-based movement, is attractive for developing countries because it is not contingent on commercial presence in the host country.

- It may be easier to create a separate fast-track non-immigration visa category for strictly temporary contract-based movement than for employment-based movement (see below).

This view has also received support from others (Winters *et al.*, 2003) who argue that subcontracting arrangements between two companies should have priority, as they may present the fewest negotiating obstacles, including because enforcement possibilities are greater (*e.g.* tracking responsibility and enforcement costs can be attributed to the beneficiaries, domestic companies).

Contractual service suppliers are currently covered in some schedules and some offers. They tend to have more restricted conditions than intra-corporate transferees, such as shorter periods of stay (*e.g.* specifications of six months or the time needed to complete the contract, whichever is shorter) and access in some sectors only. While some members do not apply economic needs tests (with some important exceptions), the possibility of quotas is indicated in some cases (in the absence of a safeguard for services, this seems to be the tradeoff for access). Some members (*e.g.* the EU) make a distinction between contractual service suppliers who are employees and those who are independent professionals, but others (*e.g.* Canada) do not. Independent professionals can be subject to more stringent conditions (*e.g.* shorter period of stay, access restricted to fewer sectors).

Some questions

However, there are a number of questions that might be raised about the above approach. The main issue, and one flagged by the authors themselves, is the difficulty of distinguishing between a contractual service supplier and employment-based movement. In some cases, persons who may be considered contractual service suppliers by some WTO members may be termed employees of the domestic company by other WTO members, in order to achieve the public policy objective of bringing them under domestic labour law.[32] In addition, given that while the person is termed an employee, he/she is generally not free to change employers without permission, it can be argued that such individuals have not genuinely entered the labour market.

Further, exclusion of foreign employees of domestic companies from the scope of mode 4 may create economic distortions. A service delivered by a foreign worker under an employment contract to a local provider may be treated differently from the same service provided by the same person acting as an unattached service provider under a consultant contract. This distinction would channel into one form of service delivery transactions that ideally should take another form (Winters *et al.*, 2001). Removing the focus from employer-based movement also effectively leaves out the main schemes operating in some WTO members, in particular the United States.

Finally, it is worth asking whether the political factors affecting employment-based movement will not eventually also apply to other types of movement. For example, if wage parity requirements are not applied to intra-corporate transferees, it could be argued that foreign established firms bringing in intra-corporate transferees might enjoy a cost advantage in bidding for outsourced work in the domestic market. Some WTO members already include some stipulations for intra-corporate transferees, *e.g.* in its schedule of commitments, Hong Kong, China, stipulates that businesses brining in intra-corporate transferees must be *bona fide* and that the number of sponsored entrants must be reasonable having regard to the size and operations of the business. Similarly, for contractual service suppliers in the new EU offer,

---

32. US labour groups insist that the Labor Condition Application – including its wage parity requirement – must be an integral part of any international agreement, and there is a strong presumption that the requirements of this measure can only be effectively policed in the context of an employment contract (Chaudhuri *et al.*, 2003).

foreign service providers are eligible to fulfil only those contracts that are subject to a tendering procedure, or at least advertised.

Key questions

o Should the focus of the GATS negotiations be the highly skilled? How far along the skill chain is it politically feasible to go?

o How should persons such as junior staff undergoing training as future managers, persons without university qualifications but with useful work experience and persons who may not be highly skilled but who possess essential technical knowledge be dealt with? Do sector-specific commitments offer a realistic option for these cases? What problems do they pose for migration authorities?

o To what extent do the current GATS commitments in terms of categories, duration of stay and type of contract, meet business requirements?

o To what extent do enforcement issues vary between different groups – contractual service suppliers, intra-corporate transferees and employment-based movement? How should the costs of enforcement be allocated?

o Are the political issues related to contractual service suppliers and intra-corporate transferees less difficult than those associated with employment-based movement?

What measures can be taken to facilitate movement under mode 4?

In an increasingly globalised world, firms need to be able to deploy personnel for short periods to meet specific project and contract requirements in different countries, often under tight deadlines. However, time-consuming and costly administrative procedures can cause problems for short-term assignments, the largest growth area of mode 4 movement.[33] Chaudhuri *et al.* (2003) highlight visa formalities as a significant obstacle to mode 4 trade.

A number of commentators have noted that these difficulties can be attributed to the lack of separation in procedures concerning temporary and permanent labour, so that applicants for temporary labour are forced to meet strict conditions and undergo procedures associated with permanent migration, although this may be neither warranted nor efficient. Proposals have been developed for a GATS visa, tailor-made for mode 4 entry, including by industry groups (*e.g.* the US Coalition of Services Industries and the European Services Forum).

Building on these proposals, Chaudhuri *et al.* (2003) propose a special service provider visa (SPV) for natural persons with professional skills on short-term, intra-company visits (category 1) and on short-term visits to fulfil

---

33. PricewaterhouseCoopers (2001) found that 42% of companies outsourced management of work permits for internationally assigned staff, with a view to increasing efficiency and reducing costs.

contracts (categories 2 and 3). In each case, the short term is defined as a stay of less than a year. Key elements of the visa are presented in Box 3.1.

Some questions

Some questions may arise about the feasibility of such a visa. First, the types of mode 4 entrants concerned – intra-corporate transferees and contractual service suppliers – may cut across several existing visa categories in some countries (see Annex B). While some countries have special visas for intra-corporate transferees, contractual service suppliers may be covered by existing visa categories (*e.g.* those covering fashion models, university lecturers). Countries may therefore be reluctant to change existing schemes, especially if they consider them a good source of more detailed information on entrants. Further, although temporary and permanent entrants are separated, no distinction is made in migration categories between service and non-service activities. Chaudhuri *et al.* (2003) acknowledge that descriptions of (temporary) immigration regimes reveal that most do not treat mode 4 as a distinct category and that this raises concerns about how any future liberalisation can be made compatible with members' migration regimes.

For countries that lack a visa system for temporary business entrants, the introduction of such a visa might be useful. However, it must be asked whether all WTO members have the capacity to introduce and administer such a scheme and whether this would represent a good use of resources for countries where entrants under the visa might be small. (There is something of a vicious circle here, as the absence of such a visa makes it very difficult to know just how many potential entrants there might be; in countries without business visas, business persons often enter as tourists).

A second concern, which the authors also acknowledge, is that special rules under temporary entry for particular groups could increase the burden on both immigration officers and business people. That is, the introduction of the SPV might expose the relevant entrants to a more detailed bureaucratic procedure than is currently the case.

Key questions

o How feasible is a service provider visa?

o How would it fit with existing visa systems in WTO members?

o What might be the implementation issues, including for countries with fewer administrative resources?

o What might be the advantages, including in terms of better measurement of, and control over, trade flows?

Box 3.1. Service provider visa

A special permit, entitled a "service provider visa" (SPV), can be obtained by nationals of other WTO members from X, when the applicant falls under categories 1, 2 and 3 (see above).

a) For natural persons falling under categories 1, 2 and 3, the SPV is extended strictly to personnel with requisite qualifications to fill positions responsible either for management of operations or provision of services at a level of complexity and specialty that require, at a minimum, a diploma or a university degree or demonstrated experience.

b) Applicants seeking a SPV under any category must fulfil certain requirements regarding the information necessary to support the application, proof of employment with current employer for categories 1 and 2, specific service contract(s) and/or invitation, and declaration of intention not to stay for a period of more than twelve months.

c) The SPV fees should reflect actual administrative costs.

d) For persons falling under categories 1, 2 and 3, the SPV is authorised for a period of three years, allowing for multiple entry, with no single stay exceeding one year.

e) For categories 1, 2 and 3, the provisions for renewal of the permit shall be based on the permit holder's continued status, defined as an employee of the same company or partnership for categories 1 and 2, and the absence of abuse of any of the conditions governing the use of the permit. SPV holders must seek renewal no later than one month from the date of expiration of the permit.

f) Wage parity is not a condition for the issuance, or apply to holders, of categories 1, 2 or 3 SPVs.

g) Permits for categories 2 and 3 are subject to the following conditions and are subject to renewal every three years:

o   All applications must be accompanied either by a copy of the contract(s) made between the employer and the client(s) in X, demonstrating terms and conditions of the contract, as well as its monetary value, or an invitation to the service provider from a potential client/industry association/professional body.

o   The SPV holder is permitted to stay in X for the duration of the contract(s), or 365 days, whichever is less. Remuneration provided under the contract(s) must specify payment to the employer alone for category 2 and to the service provider alone for category 3 as a condition for issuing the SPV.

h) Applicants under categories 1, 2 and 3 must submit information pertaining to level of education, qualifications (including professional accreditation when required in the home country), and proof of citizenship.

i) Holders of SPVs are not authorised to change their status to another non-immigrant visa category while using the SPV.

j) *Penalties.* For categories 1 and 2, abuse of the programme results in a one-year prohibition on inclusion in the programme.

./.

Box 3.1. Service provider visa (cont'd.)

k) *Special safeguards*. Where it can be established that a pattern of practice among a number of companies of another member has led to fraudulent use or misrepresentation of the SPV, the programme may be suspended for a temporary period of time, not to exceed one year, with respect to that member.

l) The SPV for categories 1 and 2 will be issued without unreasonable delay and in any event no later than three weeks following the satisfactory presentation of the documentation required by X.

m) Where the SPV is denied, the applicant will have an opportunity to appeal the decision and obtain a determination within one month from the time the appeal is lodged. SPV renewal procedures will follow the same conditions and maximum time frame for issuance or denial.

Source: Chaudhuri *et al.* (2003).

Regulatory transparency

Lack of information on opportunity and conditions for entry can also be a major obstacle to mobility and may particularly affect individual service suppliers (or small and medium-sized enterprises), as they lack the resources of large companies for learning about conditions across a range of WTO members and interacting with regulators in case of difficulties. Additionally, some mode 4 entrants, such as business visitors, may make frequent, short trips to other WTO members and thus require up-to-date information on any changes to entry procedures or requirements.

GATS commitments themselves do little to contribute to transparency as they are hard to read (in particular for non-GATS experts) and do not provide sufficiently detailed information about exactly how the promised access might be utilised. Indeed, schedules are not the most appropriate vehicles for this kind of information, given that they represent binding legal commitments, and WTO members may be reluctant to bind administrative procedures, including undertakings regarding processing times for, or costs of, applications.

Additionally, Chaudhuri *et al.* (2003) have noted that existing GATS transparency requirements[34] may not be adequate to ensure that members provide the necessary information for mode 4 access and that some additional

---

34. Article III requires members to publish promptly all measures of a general application which pertain to or affect the operation of the GATS. Members are also obliged to notify annually any new or changed laws, regulations or administrative guidelines which significantly affect trade in services covered by specific commitments. Members are also obliged to establish enquiry points to respond to requests for information from other WTO members.

requirements may be needed. It would be valuable to require members to make available, in a consolidated text, all measures that pertain to the temporary admission of natural persons and to provide information on the materials or evidence required of an applicant seeking temporary admission into their territories. Members' undertakings to provide this information could be included as additional commitments in their schedules.[35] They suggest that members commit to providing a consolidated text with the following information:

- Categories of permit and their requirements.

- Documentation required.

- Method of lodgement.

- Processing time and application fees (if any).

- Length and validity of stay.

- Possibility of and conditions for extensions (including availability of multiple entry visas).

- Rules regarding accompanying dependants.

- Review and/or appeal procedures (if any).

- Details of relevant contact points for further information (*e.g.* links to relevant government Web sites that provide more detailed information on embassies, consulates and other issuing bodies).

- Reference to any relevant immigration laws of general application (laws need not necessarily be included, but details should be given on where information on them can be found).

Chaudhuri *et al.* (2003) also suggest that members commit to granting approval of applications for temporary admission within a defined period of time. They also propose that interested parties (including trading partners) be given an opportunity for comment prior to the introduction of any new measure or alteration of existing measures pertaining to temporary movement under mode 4. However, a number of WTO members have raised questions about the possible administrative burden involved in providing prior consultation before

---

35. Additional commitments are commitments on good regulatory practices which are included in a third column (after the market access and national treatment columns) in GATS schedules of commitments. They were commonly used in the negotiations on telecommunications, where countries committed, for example, to establishing an independent telecommunications regulator.

introducing new regulations. This concern is acknowledged by the authors, who suggest that, if this were to seem overly burdensome, an alternative would be to strengthen the existing system of *ex post* notification to the WTO after the introduction of the measure.

Canada[36] has also proposed that each member provide voluntarily, and separately from its specific commitments, all relevant information sources for each of its commitments. Members would not be expected to provide the actual wording of relevant laws, regulations, policies, practices or administrative guidelines with respect to each commitment. They would simply cite the relevant parts of these instruments and other public information. This could be provided either with their initial offers or their final commitments. Canada noted that members could make additional commitments, or could simply table the related information bilaterally or multilaterally during negotiations.

Another option would be to follow the APEC model for information by creating a Web site dedicated to providing information on the conditions applying to temporary entry of service providers in WTO members. Each WTO member could provide information on the basic eligibility criteria, procedures for applying for visas, and the terms and conditions that apply to all permitted categories of mode 4 entrants. As with the APEC Web site, members would be responsible for the accuracy of their information and for ensuring that it is updated on a regular basis. Participation in this exercise may also provide useful spin-offs at the national level, as key agencies co-ordinate to provide the information, increasing policy makers' understanding of the relationship between trade commitments and immigration/labour market requirements.

Key questions

o How big a problem is the lack of transparency? To what extent will it increase meaningful and effective use of mode 4 access?

o What are the costs and implications of implementing greater transparency for migration authorities? What kinds of mechanisms could be used?

o Should members be encouraged to make additional commitments on transparency or left to provide this information on a purely voluntary basis?

---

36. See "Canada's view and proposal on transparency of horizontal mode 4 commitments", tabled at the UNCTAD Expert Meeting on Market Access Issues in Mode 4 and Effective Implementation of Article IV on Increasing Participation of Developing Countries held in Geneva on 29-31 July 2003.

References

Chanda, R. (1999), "Movement of Natural Persons and Trade in Services: Liberalising Temporary Movement of Labour under the GATS", Indian Council for Research on International Economic Relations, India, www.icrier.res.in.

Chaudhuri, S., A. Mattoo and R. Self (2003), "Liberalizing Mode 4: A Possible Approach", available at: www.oecd.org/ech/meetings/4sxm.

OECD (2001), "Service Providers on the Move: A Closer Look at Labour Mobility and the GATS", TD/TC/WP(2001)/FINAL, www.oecd.org.

PricewaterhouseCoopers (2001), *International Assignments: European Policy and Practice: Key Trends 1999/2000*.

Winters, A. (2001), "Assessing the Efficiency Gain from Further Liberalisation: A Comment", in P. Sauvé and A. Subramanian (eds.), *Efficiency, Equity and Legitimacy: The Multilateral Trading System and the Millennium*, University of Chicago Press, Chicago.

Winters, A., T. Walmsley, K.W. Zhen and R. Grynberg (2003), *Liberalising Temporary Movement of Natural Persons: An Agenda for the Development Round*, Blackwell Publishing, Oxford.

Part III

Conclusion

Part III

Chapter 4

Conclusion: Where Next?

The OECD/World Bank/IOL Seminar on Trade and Migration has taken a first step towards understanding one important relationship: where and how trade does – and does not – intersect with migration. The discussions revealed that much more work remains to be done in this area. Priorities for the future include: an improved understanding of how each of these communities conceptualises key features of temporary labour mobility and applies them in practice; identification of the positive and negative impacts of increased labour mobility and the necessary policy responses; and identification of practical ways to move forward, starting with a detailed consideration of how to build upon and improve existing systems for temporary labour mobility at the national level.

Migration is no longer an issue of relatively specialised concern but one with implications for a wide range of policy areas. There is accordingly a need for greater coherence between migration and other policies. This meeting has taken a first step towards understanding one important relationship: where and how trade does – and does not – intersect with migration. The discussions revealed that much more work remains to be done in this area. What should be the priorities for the future?

Finding the common language

Key terms and concepts are used differently by the migration and trade communities. Harmonisation may be a longer-term goal, but in the shorter term it would help to have a better understanding of how each community conceptualises key features of temporary labour mobility and applies them in practice. Further, differences exist not only between the trade and migration communities but also within the migration community itself, as there is no widely accepted set of migration definitions[37] – for example, "temporary" is treated differently by those countries that draw a distinction between temporary and permanent migrants and those that have only temporary migrants, but temporary migrants who can remain in the country for extended (20-year) periods. As this illustrates, attempts to clarify terminology quickly reveal fundamental national differences in approaches to migration.

Clarifying the terminology is like to entail discussion of the dividing line (if one can be drawn) between trade and migration in terms of movement related to the supply of a service on a contractual basis and movement related to employment in the domestic market of the receiving country. Disagreement over the extent to which the latter is covered by GATS mode 4 in turn rapidly leads the debate into a host of other policy areas: from whether employees of domestic companies actually become residents of the host countries from a migration and balance of payments perspective and what this means for their inclusion as a type of trade; through economic arguments about what constitutes the supply of a service in a world of outsourcing and fragmented production chains; to labour market issues about how different contractual and employment relations are treated for the purposes of domestic labour law.

Reaching a practical and constructive understanding of the scope of mode 4 is thus not something that can be achieved by the trade community alone. It will require the collective efforts of the trade, labour and migration communities. GATS mode 4 and its key constituent concepts – temporary, service, supplier (employee, contractual) – do not exist in a vacuum, but in the real world; the definition of GATS mode 4 must be workable in the context of the actual practices of governments.

Understanding the potential impacts – positive and negative – and developing appropriate complementary policies

The second challenge is to identify the positive and negative impacts of increased labour mobility and the policy responses to manage these impacts for the benefit of countries of origin and destination, as well as for individual migrants.

More work is needed to enable the making of informed choices about labour mobility. As for other areas of trade or public policy, reliable estimates of expected benefits and costs should form the basis for assessing

---

37. See International Organization for Migration (2003), World Migration 2003: *Managing Migration: Challenges and Responses for People on the Move*, Chapter 1.

the kinds of initiatives and tradeoffs that would best contribute to increasing global and national welfare. Moreover, as migration is ultimately about the lives of human beings, consideration needs to be given to the social as well as economic implications of increased labour mobility. While there is a vast literature on migration, less work has been done specifically on measuring the economic and social impacts of the kinds of temporary labour mobility that would fall under GATS mode 4.

A key question for future research is whether, or the extent to which, the challenges and impacts of the temporary labour movement envisaged by GATS mode 4 differ from permanent or indeed from other forms of temporary migration. While the potential social impact may be less than for permanent migration, the labour market impact of temporary labour mobility, combined with new general trends towards outsourcing and use of contract labour, may be greater or may pose new and different challenges for labour market regulators. Further, as emerged clearly in the meeting, concerns and impacts can also vary considerably for more highly skilled and lower-skilled labour. More empirical and analytical work is also needed to assess whether liberalising temporary labour mobility promises gains that are greater or smaller than those from liberalising other forms of trade. This is a major area for future research and one that will require the expertise of both migration and trade economists.

Only through a better understanding of the actual impact of mode 4 can the sorts of complementary policies needed to manage those impacts for the benefit of countries of origin and destination as well as for individual migrants be designed. There is considerable practical experience, and much analytical work under way, to draw upon in terms of how best to harness remittances for development, how to create a symbiotic link between mode 4 exports and other exports of services and goods and how to manage the impact of temporary foreign workers on the labour market over the longer term. Specific attention will need to be given to ensuring that developing countries are well placed to manage the impact of movement on their economies. Technical assistance and capacity building will be important in this regard.

Identifying practical ways to facilitate movement

Finally, armed with sound analysis of the potential benefits and downsides, and the policies needed to manage them, it will be necessary to take a practical approach to identifying how to move forward on labour mobility. A sensible place to start would be a detailed consideration of how best to build upon and improve existing systems for temporary labour mobility at the national level.

Where no visa systems exist to cover temporary labour mobility of the kind envisaged by GATS mode 4, introduction of a GATS visa might make sense. However, for countries that already have a range of schemes catering to a wide range of temporary workers, the additional benefits of a GATS visa need to be carefully evaluated. Indeed, there may be a risk of undermining the flexibility in existing schemes as well as undermining sources of more detailed data for a wider variety of policy purposes. In these cases, it might make more sense to treat a GATS visa as a model for certain conditions (*e.g.* regarding duration of stay or renewal procedures) to existing visas – a way of improving the conditions of relevant existing visa categories and addressing some of the enforcement concerns.

Translating existing temporary labour movement schemes into GATS commitments poses major challenges. While trade commitments are all about predictability, migration schemes put a premium on flexibility. Insistence upon binding existing access for temporary workers under GATS mode 4 may lead to commitments only at a level that can be comfortably guaranteed into the future. There are at least two ways to deal with this. One option is to explore whether there is any scope in the GATS for mechanisms that might assuage the concerns of migration regulators (especially regarding flexibility), while still meeting the desire of business for the predictability afforded by GATS commitments. Work could explore whether there is scope for a more flexible type of commitment, a kind of "soft binding" for mode 4, and what this would mean in terms of the architecture of the agreement. Alternatively, bindings may be deemed to be less important at this stage than making progress on the ground, and it is possible that increased mobility will itself create new circumstances under which liberalisation will become progressively harder to reverse as a matter of good economic policy, regardless of GATS commitments.

A similar pragmatism may be necessary with regard to lower-skilled labour. Given the greater concerns about competition with nationals, particularly those in the most vulnerable sections of society, bound commitments in the WTO on lower-skilled labour pose significant political difficulties in the short to medium term. However, there may be scope for progress via bilateral labour agreements. These agreements are a second-best solution, but they nonetheless represent an avenue for lower-skilled labour to move under conditions of legal certainty in the short to medium term. In the future, they might even be attached to regional trade agreements and thus encompass a broader range of countries. In the short term, they have certain advantages: they can serve as a useful testing ground for the design of a range of co-operative approaches and incentives for ensuring return and enforcement; and they allow for addressing specific concerns and conditions in a way not adequately addressed by GATS commitments alone.

For example, countries can use bilateral labour agreements to negotiate standards to protect workers who are particularly vulnerable to exploitation or to negotiate with recipient countries investment in training programmes in order to help increase the supply of appropriately qualified workers in shortage areas and militate against brain drain. From the point of view of WTO rules, however, bilateral labour agreements pose a challenge: they may not be consistent with MFN, and new agreements would not be covered by existing MFN exemptions. Again, a pragmatic rather than legalistic approach may be appropriate in the short term.

While sensitivities and difficulties surround the issue of temporary labour mobility, there is a strong case for moving forward. There is a lot to build upon. A certain amount of movement is already under way, with temporary movement in particular increasing rapidly. Countries have already launched regional and national initiatives to encourage mobility; global business will continue to search the global market for skills and to recruit internationally. Against this background, global trade negotiations create the requisite sense of urgency to get different parts of government to work together to identify options and solutions. There is too much at stake, for both developing and developed countries, for the trade and migration communities not to begin to undertake the serious work required to map out the way forward for global labour mobility.

Annex A

A Quick Guide to the GATS and Mode 4

This annex aims at facilitating the understanding of the GATS and mode 4. It introduces the GATS and mode 4, summarising for each the scope of application and functioning. It also reviews the state of current negotiations for further services trade liberalisation.

BACKGROUND

What is the GATS?

The General Agreement on Trade in Services (GATS) is a multilaterally agreed framework agreement for trade in services which applies to all 148 WTO members. It has three main objectives:

- *To progressively liberalise trade in services* through successive rounds of negotiations which should aim at promoting the interests of all members of the WTO and achieving an overall balance of rights and obligations.

- *To encourage economic growth and development* through liberalisation of trade in services, as the General Agreement on Tariffs and Trade (GATT) does through the liberalisation of trade in goods.

- *To increase the participation of developing countries in world trade in services* and expand their services exports by developing their export capacity and securing export opportunities in sectors of export interest to them.

The agreement has a wide scope and applies to all services supplied on a commercial basis. It excludes most air transport services as well as services supplied in the exercise of governmental authority (defined as services supplied neither on a commercial basis nor in competition with one or more service suppliers).

The agreement includes both rules and a framework for countries to make commitments to open particular service sectors to foreign suppliers. These market opening commitments are referred to as "specific commitments" and set out the service sectors in which foreign suppliers will be permitted and the conditions under which they will be permitted.

Accordingly, the GATS is divided in two parts. The first part consists of general obligations, as well as some obligations which apply only where commitments for particular sectors are made. An example of a general obligation is the "most favoured nation" or MFN requirement, which requires WTO members to treat all other WTO members as well as they treat their most favoured WTO member. That is, treatment offered to one WTO member must be extended to all other members. (There are some exceptions, see Box A.1 below.)

Some transparency requirements are also general obligations (e.g. the requirement to publish or otherwise make publicly available at the national level all relevant measures of general application which pertain to the agreement). Other transparency requirements apply only where a commitment has been made (e.g. the requirement to notify other WTO members via the WTO Council for Trade in Services[38] of any new law or any changes to existing laws, etc., which significantly affect trade in services covered by a commitment). Another example of these types of obligations is the requirement that, in sectors where specific commitments are undertaken, measures of general application affecting trade in services are to be administered in a reasonable, objective and impartial manner (Article VI.1).

The second part of the GATS sets out the framework under which countries decide which service sectors they want to allow foreign suppliers to enter, and under what conditions. The commitments made under this framework are referred to as "specific commitments". The commitments undertaken by each WTO member are contained in individual schedules of commitments which are annexed to the GATS. The text of the GATS and the schedules of commitments for each WTO member are available on the WTO Web site at www.wto.org.

For the purpose of making commitments, a list of 12 service sectors and around 160 subsectors was developed. The Services Sectoral Classification List (MTN.GNS.W/120, known as "W/120") includes cross-references to the

---

38. The Council for Trade in Services is a body made up of representatives of all WTO members. It normally meets around four times a year. The WTO Secretariat Trade in Services Division serves as the Secretariat to that body and its subsidiary bodies: the Working Party on Domestic Regulation; the Committee on Financial Services; the Working Party on GATS Rules; and the Committee on Specific Commitments.

United Nations Central Product Classification (Provisional CPC). While its use is not obligatory, many WTO members have used W/120 in making their GATS specific commitments.

As a further tool for making market-opening commitments, the GATS also sets out four possible modes, or ways, in which services can be traded between WTO members. In mode 1 (cross-border supply), the service crosses the border (*e.g.* a Mexican architect faxes a plan to a client in Japan). In mode 2 (consumption abroad), the service is consumed in the territory of the service supplier (*e.g.* a Mexican tourist goes to Japan for a holiday; a ship pulls into a foreign port for repairs). In mode 3 (commercial presence), the service supplier establishes a commercial presence in another WTO member to provide the service (*e.g.* a Mexican architecture firm opens a branch in Japan). In mode 4, an individual service supplier moves temporarily to another WTO member for the purposes of supplying a service (*e.g.* a Mexican architect visits Japan for six months to supervise the construction of the building she designed).

Mode 3 and mode 4 are, in a sense, counterparts. When the agreement was being negotiated, developed countries argued for the inclusion of investment in services (*i.e.* movement of capital); in response, developing countries insisted on similar treatment for movement of labour. This led to the inclusion of "commercial presence" (mode 3) and "presence of natural persons" (mode 4) in the agreement (Mattoo, 2003).

What is mode 4?

The movement of labour from a country can vary in several ways: length of stay, level of skills and nature of the contract. A person can move for one day or permanently; be relatively unskilled or be a specialist in a particular field; move as an independent professional or be transferred from company headquarters in one country to a branch office in another country (Mattoo, 2003). The question of which aspects of these variations are covered by GATS mode 4 is discussed below.

Who is included in mode 4?

Technically, mode 4 is defined in Article I.2(d) of the GATS as being "the supply of a service… by a service supplier of one member, through presence of natural persons of a member in the territory of another member". This definition applies to nationals as well as, under certain circumstances, to permanent residents, of WTO members seeking to supply services abroad (permanent residents are covered where the member does not have nationals or accords substantially the same treatment to permanent residents and nationals) [Article XXVIII(k)].

Further elaboration is provided in the GATS Annex on Movement of Natural Person Supplying Services under the Agreement. The Annex applies to "measures affecting natural persons who are service suppliers of a member, and natural persons of a member who are employed by a service supplier of a member, in respect of the supply of a service". The first category is clear: "natural persons who are service suppliers of a member" covers self-employed or independent service suppliers who obtain their remuneration directly from customers. However, there is some confusion about what is covered by the second category ("natural persons of a member who are employed by a service supplier of a member").

The WTO Secretariat background note on mode 4 (1998) notes that this wording could be read to suggest that foreigners *employed by host country companies* are also included under mode 4. However, as Article I.2(d) seems to cover only *foreign employees of foreign firms established in another member*, the Secretariat background note suggests that foreigners working for host country companies would fall under GATS mode 4 if they worked on a contractual basis as independent suppliers for a locally owned firm, but would not necessarily seem to be covered if they were employees of that firm.

Nonetheless, a number of GATS specific commitments (*i.e.* the market opening commitments made by WTO members) actually refer to short-term *employment*. As specific commitments also form an integral part of the GATS, there is thus a certain degree of legal uncertainty with regard to coverage (Karsenty, 2000). This situation can be further complicated by the fact that some WTO members deem almost all types of foreign temporary workers to be employees for the purposes of bringing them under domestic labour law (with implications for their wages, conditions and social protection).

Generally, GATS mode 4 is seen as covering:

- Persons providing services when a foreign service supplier obtains a contract to supply services to the host country company and sends its employees to provide the services.

- Independent service providers abroad: an individual selling services to a host country company or to an individual.

- Persons employed abroad by foreign companies established in the host country (but excluding nationals of the host country).

What is temporary?

Mode 4 encompasses natural persons providing services in any of the service sectors on a "temporary" or non-permanent basis. However, further clarification may also be required on the issue of "temporary". There is no standard definition of temporary in the GATS and, for the purposes of specific commitments, WTO members are free to interpret the term as they wish and to set varying definitions for different categories of service providers. In practice, many WTO members' specific commitments distinguish between:

- "Business visitors", *i.e.* short-term stays of a few months (often limited to three months), with no remuneration received in the host country.

- Temporary movements of between a few months and a few years, including:

  - Existing employees transferred within the same foreign controlled company (intra-corporate transferees, generally limited to 2-5 years).

  - Service suppliers on specific term contracts with foreign or nationally owned firms.

  - Self-employed service providers whose remuneration is wholly or only partly received in the host country (Arkell, 1998).

While "temporary" is not defined positively in the GATS, it is defined negatively, *i.e.* permanent migration is explicitly excluded. The Annex on Movement of Natural Persons Supplying Services under the Agreement states that the GATS does not apply to measures affecting individuals seeking access to the employment markets of a member or to measures regarding citizenship, residence or employment on a permanent basis. The Annex also states that, regardless of their obligations under the Agreement, members are free to regulate the entry and stay of individuals in their territory provided that the measures concerned "are not applied in such a manner as to nullify or impair the benefits accruing to any member under the terms of a specific commitment". The existence of visa requirements for natural persons from some members but not others is not *per se* regarded as nullifying or impairing such benefits.

However, some commentators have queried the GATS distinction between service providers and persons entering the labour market in a country. They argue that, given that temporary entry under GATS commitments can last for up to three years (and in some cases longer), the service provider has in effect entered the local labour market, even though he/she is not applying for citizenship, as she/he is providing a service which a local person could probably do (Young, 2000).

What is a service supplier?

The GATS only covers services and service suppliers, but it may not always be easy to know what constitutes the supply of a service. For example, should fruit pickers be viewed as temporary agricultural labourers (outside the scope of mode 4) or as suppliers of fruit-picking services? The answer may in part depend upon how broadly WTO members interpret the scope of the category "services incidental to agriculture" in the Services Sectoral Classification List (W/120).

Also, tasks performed on a fee or contract basis, without ownership of the input or output, are sometimes deemed to be services, even when they would appear technically to be manufacturing in nature. For example, a factory which receives a ream of fabric and a contract to sew 300 shirts is a supplier of tailoring services, whereas a factory which owns the cloth and produces 300 shirts which it then sells under its own mark is a textile manufacturer. In the world of increased outsourcing of activities along the production chain, there is some debate over to the extent to which activities previously classified as manufacturing can now be broken down into, and classified as, services. There is thus some scope for differing interpretations of what constitutes a service.[39]

Further, while mode 4 technically includes service suppliers at all skill levels, in practice WTO members' commitments have been generally limited to the higher skilled – managers, executives, specialists – although these terms are generally not further defined.

Summary

While there is no single, clear definition of mode 4, a useful approach might be to consider both *duration* and *purpose* of stay. That is, mode 4 service suppliers:

- Gain entry for a specific purpose (to fulfil a service contract as self-employed or an employee of a foreign service supplier).

- Are normally confined to one sector (as opposed to workers who enter under general migration or asylum programmes who can move between sectors).

- Are temporary (*i.e.* they are neither migrating on a permanent basis nor seeking entry to the labour market).

These elements, however imperfect, could help to distinguish mode 4 temporary service suppliers from wider groups of temporary workers (Table A.1).

---

39. It has been questioned whether it makes sense, including in terms of the commercial reality of firms supplying both goods and services, to limit labour mobility solely to service suppliers (Feketekuty, 2000). Indeed, a growing number of regional trade agreements apply mobility provisions not only to service suppliers, but also to providers of goods and investors.

Table A.1. Summary of mode 4 coverage

Included	Excluded	Differences of view exist
Temporary movement (temporary is undefined)	Permanent migration (residence, citizenship or employment on a permanent basis)	
Related to the supply of services	Persons working in non-service sectors, *e.g.* agriculture, manufacturing	Scope of activities included in "services incidental to agriculture" (*e.g.* temporary agricultural workers or suppliers of fruit-picking services?) or "services incidental to manufacturing"
All skill levels included (but in practice commitments to date are limited to the highly skilled)		
Foreign employees of foreign companies established in the host country	Domestic (nationals of host country) employees of foreign companies established in the host country	Foreign employees of domestic companies
Business visitors Intra-corporate transferees Contractual service suppliers (self-employed or as employee of a foreign service supplier)	Persons seeking to enter the employment market	

How does the GATS operate?

What is a commitment?

GATS commitments are the guaranteed minimum treatment offered to other WTO members; countries are always free to offer better treatment if they wish, but they cannot offer worse. Commitments are binding, *i e.* they cannot be changed without paying compensation to other members (this takes the form of a commitment for access in another area of equal value to the one being changed or withdrawn). Commitments are also MFN, *i.e.* the access offered is open to suppliers from all other WTO members (a country cannot offer access to suppliers from some WTO members and not others, subject to the exceptions set out below).

Commitments can be made for each sector or subsector and, within this, for each mode of supply. For example, under "legal services", commitments can be made for "foreign legal consultants", with some access granted under mode 3 and mode 4, but not mode 1. Alternatively, commitments can be made "horizontally", covering a single mode of supply across all sectors listed in the schedule. Horizontal commitments apply to all sectors listed in the schedule unless otherwise clearly specified at the sectoral level (*e.g.* a country's schedule specifies that its horizontal mode 4 commitment does not apply to legal services). Most commitments for movement of service suppliers under mode 4 are horizontal rather than sectoral, reflecting existing migration regimes.[40]

What are market access and national treatment?

For each service sector or subsector, and for each mode of supply within that, countries make commitments as to the level of "market access" and "national treatment" they will offer. Read together, market access and national treatment commitments inform a foreign supplier about the access they will have to the WTO member's market and any special conditions that will apply to them as foreigners. In making commitments, a WTO member has three main choices:

- A commitment to provide full market access and/or national treatment for a particular mode – *i.e.* to maintain no restrictions – indicated in the schedule by "None".

- No commitment to provide anything on national treatment and/or market access for a particular mode; this is indicated by "Unbound" (*i.e.* no bound commitment undertaken).

- Partial commitments for market access and/or national treatment, with the remaining restrictions listed in the schedule.

There are six types of restrictions on access to their market for a given service that countries need to list in their commitment if they want to use them. These restrictions can apply to both nationals and foreigners or only to foreigners. These *market access* restrictions are:

- Restrictions on the number of service suppliers, including in the form of monopolies or exclusive service suppliers.

- Restrictions on the total value of service transactions or assets.

- Restrictions on the total number of service operations or the total quantity of service output.

- Restrictions on the total number of natural persons that may be employed in a particular service sector or that a service supplier may employ.

---

40. It should be noted that a WTO member's mode 4 commitments cover the acceptance of foreign service suppliers into its territory, not the sending of its own nationals abroad as service suppliers.

- Restrictions on or requirements for certain types of legal entity or joint venture for the supply of a service.

- Limitations on the participation of foreign capital in terms of maximum percentage limit on foreign shareholding or the total value of individual or aggregate foreign investment.

National treatment means that foreign services and service suppliers are granted treatment no less favourable than that accorded to like national services and service suppliers. This can mean formally identical or formally different treatment – the key requirement is that it does not modify the conditions of competition in favour of services or service suppliers who are nationals instead of foreigners. National treatment can also cover both *de jure* and *de facto* discrimination; that is, even if a measure applies to both foreigners and nationals it may still be discriminatory if its *effect* is to discriminate against foreign suppliers. However, national treatment does not require a member to compensate for any inherent competitive disadvantage which results from the foreign character of the relevant service or service suppliers.

A key consideration in national treatment is whether the services or service suppliers are "like". The GATS, like other WTO agreements, does not define "like", and panels under the WTO dispute settlement system have tended to approach the issue of "likeness" on a case-by-case basis, taking into account, *inter alia*, consumer perceptions of the degree to which a particular good is "like", and its substitutability.

WTO members are free to make no commitment on national treatment, or to provide partial national treatment provided they list the measures they maintain that discriminate in favour of nationals in their schedule. Unlike the situation for market access, there is no specific list of the types of measures that have to be scheduled; members must judge whether a measure breaches national treatment and should therefore be scheduled. A measure may not be considered discriminatory if it is genuinely open to both national and foreigners to fulfil its conditions, *e.g.* a requirement for a degree of proficiency in a certain language need not be discriminatory if it is genuinely possible for foreigners to be able to learn the language and achieve the required level of proficiency. Some examples of the types of measures which would need to be listed in the schedule as limitations on national treatment include: eligibility for subsidies reserved to nationals; the ability to lease or own land reserved to nationals; and citizenship requirements for professionals.

What are the options in making commitments?

In making commitments, WTO members have a number of choices:

- They can exclude an entire sector (*e.g.* health services) or parts of a sector (*e.g.* everything other than general nursing) from their commitments. WTO members are free to define the sector as they wish; they can refer to a list developed for the GATS negotiations (the Services Sectoral Classification List, see above) or to the United Nations Central Product Classification to which this GATS list refers, or they can use their own definitions.

- They can exclude some modes of supply. For example, a WTO member may decide to permit its nationals to study abroad (mode 2) but not to permit foreign university lecturers to teach in its territory (mode 4).

- They can place limits on the "market access" they offer (*e.g.* they can limit the number and type of foreign computer professionals and the activities in which they can engage).

- They can discriminate against foreign providers in favour of nationals (*e.g.* by placing additional conditions or requirements on foreign computer professionals or restricting some activities or benefits to national computer professionals).

- They can discriminate among foreign suppliers (*i.e.* they can give better treatment to suppliers from some countries) if they have an MFN exemption for the relevant service. Countries had a one-off opportunity to claim exemptions from MFN at the time they joined the GATS (information on MFN exemptions related to mode 4 is included in Box A.1 and Table A.1). Countries that are a party to regional trade agreements are also able to discriminate in favour of other members of those agreements.

- They can commit to providing less access than they currently actually provide (*e.g.* a country may commit in the GATS to allowing 40 000 foreign professionals to provide services temporarily each year, but may in practice under their national law allow 100 000 to enter). Because a commitment is a binding guarantee of minimum treatment, countries often commit to less than they currently offer to leave themselves room to manoeuvre (in the example above, to change the national law to drop the number from 100 000 to 50 000) Indeed, many current GATS commitments represent significantly less openness than actually exists in the country concerned.

- They can commit to liberalise at a chosen future date to give themselves time to ensure that the necessary regulatory framework is in place (*e.g.* they can commit to allowing foreign lawyers to work in their territory, but only from 2010).

- Developing countries have additional flexibility to liberalise fewer sectors and to attach conditions to the access offered. Moreover, other members should facilitate their participation in trade, including by liberalising modes and sectors of interest to them, and should establish special contact points to provide information to developing country service suppliers.

What has been achieved so far on mode 4?

Even by the modest standards of services liberalisation in the Uruguay Round, little was done on liberalising the temporary movement of service suppliers. Most countries made only limited commitments on mode 4. GATS commitments are also guaranteed *minimum* treatment, so countries tended to be conservative, with most committing to a more restrictive regime than they were – or are – actually employing. Key features of the commitments on mode 4 are outlined in Box A.1.

Against this backdrop, expectations are running high among some WTO members for more meaningful progress on mode 4 in the current round of services negotiations. The structure of those negotiations, and the progress to date on mode 4, is outlined below.

THE CURRENT NEGOTIATIONS

The story so far…

1 January 2000: The negotiations commence

The services negotiations formally commenced on 1 January 2000. Even though the 1999 WTO Ministerial Conference in Seattle had failed to launch a broader round of trade negotiations, new negotiations on services and agriculture were already mandated under the agreements reached in the Uruguay Round. For services, this mandate is contained in GATS Article XIX, which requires members to enter into successive rounds of negotiations, the first beginning not later than five years from date of entry into force of the WTO (*i.e.* from 1 January 1995).

Box A.1. What is the current picture for mode 4 commitments?

Skill levels. While mode 4 technically covers all skill levels, commitments are generally limited to the more highly skilled (managers, executives, specialists). The majority of commitments concern executives, managers and specialists, with around half relating explicitly to intra-corporate transferees. Only 17% of all horizontal entries cover low-skilled personnel (*e.g.* "business sellers") and only ten countries have allowed some form of restricted entry to "other level" personnel (Chanda, 1999). Further, general terms used in commitments, such as "managers" or "business visitors", are not defined, leaving considerable scope for interpretation and discretionary action by officials.

Horizontal rather than sectoral commitments. Commitments on mode 4 generally apply the same conditions to all service sectors, with no greater access given in sectors of particular relevance to mode 4 (*e.g.* professional services). Most of these horizontal commitments generally take the form of "unbound except for..." and then state special access conditions for particular types of labour (level of skill, type of occupation) and purpose of their movement (*e.g.* establishing a commercial presence).

More restrictive. Fewer commitments have been made in mode 4 than for other modes of supply by both developed and developing countries. There are very few cases of full commitments, and fewer cases of partial commitments, than for other modes of supply. Overall, developed countries have scheduled commitments in 50% of service sectors and developing countries in 11% of service sectors, but sectors in which mode 4 is important (*e.g.* professional and health services) tend to have fewer commitments.

Length of stay. There is no standard definition of what classifies as "temporary" movement. Only about one-third of commitments include any specified duration of stay and these are mostly for intra-corporate transferees (generally 2-5 years) and business visitors (generally three months).

Economic needs tests (ENTs). Economic needs or labour market tests are found in 50 cases. They are mostly scheduled as part of horizontal commitments (sector-specific ENTs appear in medical, dental and hospital, entertaining and financial services) and generally apply to specialist personnel, highly qualified professionals, managers and executives. In all, 23 countries have made commitments that, for certain categories of natural persons, ENTs will *not* apply (generally those related to mode 3 establishment and to persons holding management positions or experts with specialised knowledge of the company). Few countries comply with the requirement for information as to ENT criteria.

Other restrictions. These include: quotas on the number of foreign suppliers, the proportion of total employment met by foreigners or the proportion of senior staff (80 cases); pre-employment requirements (*i.e.* the person must already be employed, over 100 cases); technology transfer requirements (*i.e.* training of local staff, mainly included by developing countries, 32 cases); restrictions on geographic and sectoral mobility or mobility between firms (10 cases).

Box A.1. What is the current picture for mode 4 commitments? (cont'd.)

MFN exemptions. There are 38 MFN exemptions relevant to mode 4, of which 32 are preferential agreements and the rest are reciprocal (or, in two cases, preferential and reciprocal, see Annex A.1). Where measures have been specified in detail, they relate, for example, to granting of work permits, waiving of ENTs or improved access for certain activities. Beneficiary countries covered are not always identified, but factors listed include traditional sources of supply, geographical zones, regional organisations and language.

Wage parity and strike clauses. Conditions relating to domestic wage legislation, working hours and social security have been scheduled by 50 countries (this does not include general references to domestic legislation, and there may be more members with such requirements in practice). In 22 cases, countries have reserved the right to suspend commitments in the event of a labour dispute (this seems to apply mainly to intra-corporate transferees at senior levels).

Source: WTO Secretariat, 1998; Chanda, 1999; Young, 2000.

March 2001: The negotiating guidelines agreed

GATS Article XIX also requires members to establish negotiating guidelines and procedures for each round of services negotiations. In March 2001, WTO members reached agreement on guidelines for the current negotiations. Separate guidelines covering least developed countries (LDCs) were finalised in September 2003 (see Annex A.2).[41] These guidelines note that LDCs have identified movement of natural persons as service suppliers under GATS mode 4 as important to them and state that members shall, to the extent possible, consider undertaking commitments to provide access, taking into account all categories of natural persons identified by LDCs in their request.

December 2002: The WTO Ministerial Conference in Doha

The Doha Development Agenda (DDA) endorsed the work already undertaken, reaffirmed the negotiating guidelines and procedures, and established some key elements of the timetable for the negotiations. These were:

- Deadline for the submission of initial requests for specific commitments: 30 June 2002.

- Deadline for the submission of initial offers for specific commitments: 31 March 2003.

---

41. While developing countries self-select in the WTO, LDC status is based on inclusion in the United Nations list of 50 LDCs.

- Stock taking on all GATS-related matters: WTO Ministerial Conference, Cancun 2003.

- Overall deadline for the negotiations: 1 January 2005, as part of the DDA single undertaking.

Two terms need a short explanation. First, the word "initial" reflects the reality that the negotiating process is a succession of requests and offers (see Box A.2 for an explanation of the request-offer process). Initial requests are not necessarily exhaustive and countries can come back with further requests at a later stage. Moreover, an initial offer can be subject to change, *i.e.* it can be scaled up or down, with members remaining free to withdraw their initial offer at any stage during the negotiations. Individual WTO members are also under no obligation to make either requests or offers in the negotiations.

Second, the term "single undertaking" means that all negotiating subjects are concluded as part of a single package at the same time. The idea of a single undertaking is to help all countries find a balance of interests in the outcome of negotiations, with countries able to balance concessions granted in some areas against gains made in other areas.

10-14 September 2003: The WTO Ministerial Conference in Cancun

With the failure of the WTO Ministerial in Cancun, the overall deadline of the DDA negotiations of 1 January 2005 now looks unlikely to be met. Much will depend on whether efforts to restart the negotiations in the coming months meet with success.

What is on the table on mode 4 in the GATS negotiations?

Phase one: general negotiating proposals

In the first phase of the negotiations – roughly between their commencement on 1 January 2000 and the WTO Ministerial in Doha in 2002 – a number of members tabled general proposals outlining their interests in the services negotiations (these proposals are all available at www.wto.org). Out of a total of approximately 126 proposals, six were tabled on mode 4 by Canada, Colombia, the European Communities and its member states, India, Japan and the United States (mode 4 was also included in a general proposal from Kenya).

These proposals contain a number of ideas about how to improve mode 4. Most ideas either seek to increase market access (mostly developing country proposals) or to increase the effectiveness of existing market access (supported by most major developed countries). The main ideas include:

- *Greater clarity and predictability in WTO members' commitments, e.g.* by: *i)* agreeing common definitions for the main categories of personnel included in many WTO members' commitments, including by reference to the International Standard Classification of Occupations (ISCO-88); many members refer to "executives, managers, specialists", but there is no common understanding of who is covered by these categories; and *ii)* providing information on economic needs tests (*i.e.* where entry of foreigners is subject to an assessment of needs in the domestic market), such as the criteria used, the responsible authorities, the likely time frame for determinations and a record of recent decisions.

- *Greater transparency*: existing access is not always used because service suppliers lack information on the necessary requirements and procedures. WTO members could provide one-stop information on all relevant procedures and requirements via a dedicated Web site covering all WTO members, via notifications to the WTO, or via a one-stop contact point at the national level. Other suggestions include prior consultation on regulatory changes, timely responses to applications and the right of appeal.

- *GATS visa*: to facilitate entry of mode 4 service suppliers and avoid the detailed visa procedures currently required in many countries (often not separated from permanent migration). The visa would be issued rapidly, time-limited, cover both independent service suppliers and intra-corporate transferees, include appeal rights and be backed up by a bond, with sanctions for abuse.

- *More market access*: *i)* commitments for particular service sectors in high demand (*e.g.* information and communications technology, professional services) rather than the current standard treatment for mode 4 entry across all sectors; *ii)* better access for some groups, in particular intra-corporate transferees, via "blanket" applications by companies or by charging companies for streamlined processing (including via a GATS visa); *iii)* more access for other types of skilled, but not necessarily highly skilled, personnel such as "technical support personnel" or "non-professional essential personnel" or for trainees (future executives).

Phase two: requests and offers

To date, *initial requests* have been received from about 35 WTO members. As requests are communicated between the WTO members concerned (see Box A.2) and do not go through the WTO Secretariat, there is no central collection point for requests. It is therefore not possible to have an exact number of requests or to have an overview of their content. While some WTO members have made their requests – or summaries of their requests – public, others have chosen not to. It is the decision of individual WTO members whether or not to make their initial requests public.

Some WTO members issue summaries of the requests they receive. For example, the European Communities and its member states has indicated that over half the requests it has received from developing countries include reference to mode 4; and that of the 26 requests it has received on mode 4, 24 came from developing countries. It also has its own offensive interests in mode 4, and has made requests of Ecuador, India, Peru, Malaysia, Morocco and the Philippines, as well as other developing countries, to improve their commitments under mode 4 (Niessen, 2003).

In terms of *initial offers*, to date, 37 WTO members have submitted initial offers. They are: Argentina; Australia; Bahrain; Bolivia; Canada; Chile; China; Chinese Taipei; Colombia; Czech Republic; European Communities and its member states; Fiji; Guatemala; Hong Kong, China; Iceland; Israel; Japan; Korea; Liechtenstein; Macao, China; Mexico; New Zealand; Norway; Panama; Paraguay; Peru; Poland; Singapore; Slovak Republic; Slovenia; Sri Lanka; St Kitts and Nevis; Switzerland; Thailand; Turkey; United States and Uruguay.

Of these offers, 12 have been derestricted by the member concerned and are publicly available on the WTO Web site (in the TN/S/O document series).[42] Six others are available via national or other Web sites.[43] It is the decision of the individual member whether or not to make their initial offer public.

---

42. As at 29 October, offers were available in this series from: Australia, Canada, Chile, the European Communities and its member states, Iceland, Japan, Liechtenstein, New Zealand, Norway, Slovenia, Turkey and the United States.

43. Additionally, on the Internet offers from Argentina; Hong Kong, China; Panama; Paraguay; Switzerland and Uruguay have been located.

Of the 18 offers which were publicly available, offers on mode 4 have been made by nine WTO members: Argentina; Canada; the European Communities and its member states; Hong Kong, China; Japan; New Zealand; Norway; Slovenia and Switzerland. Highlights include:

- *Argentina*: Additional categories have been added for business people, professionals and specialists and for representatives of foreign enterprises. Managers, executives and specialists have been brought under the heading of "intra-corporate transferees". Additional commitments have been made for all these groups, noting the possibility of granting multiple entries. Business people cannot receive remuneration in Argentina or directly sell services to the public and are granted 90-day stays, extendable for a further 90 days. Professionals and specialists are either: *i)* persons carrying out professional or technical activities irrespective of whether or not these are remunerative, who are granted a stay of 15 days, extendable for a further 15 days; or *ii)* persons providing services to a natural or juridical person in Argentina as permanent employees or freelancers, who have a one-year stay, extendable for further one-year periods as long as they remain contracted employees. Similar conditions apply to managers, executives and specialists entering as intra-corporate transferees. Representatives of foreign enterprises are persons who receive remuneration from abroad; they cannot provide services in Argentina under a contract which links them to an enterprise established in Argentina. They are granted stays of one year, extendable for further one-year periods for as long as they retain the status of contracted employee.

- *Canada*: Business visitors are now admitted to supply after-sale and after-lease services and labour market tests are not required. Entry and stay is specified as being for a period of up to six months with the possibility of extensions. Intra-corporate transferees must now have been employed for one year within the immediately preceding three-year period. Definitions of executives, managers and specialists have been clarified. Labour market tests have been removed for intra-corporate transferees, but work permits are required. The period of stay for managers and executives is equivalent to the period of transfer, with extensions possible provided temporary residency status is maintained and demonstrated. Similar conditions apply for specialists, but the entry and stay, including extensions, must not exceed five years. Conditions have also been clarified for professionals, who are no longer subject to labour market tests. Work permits are required and period of stay is for an initial period of one year or the time necessary to complete the contract, whichever is less, although extensions are possible. There is a limit of ten senior computer specialists per project. Spouses and common-law partners of qualifying intra-corporate transferees or professionals are a new category and are not subject to labour market tests.

- *European Communities and its member states*: Additional horizontal and sector-specific commitments. Definitions of intra-corporate transferees are clarified and extended to include graduate trainees (persons with a university degree transferring for career development or training purposes). Business visitors in certain categories are permitted for a stay of up to 90 days in any 12-month period without application of an economic needs test. Certain restrictions are removed for individual member states. In the category of contractual service suppliers, employees of juridical persons are permitted stays of up to six months (cumulative) in any 12-month period. Contracts may be for up to 12 months. Qualification requirements apply, as well as at least three years of professional experience in the sector. Additional sectors have been included such as book-keeping services, related scientific and technical consulting services, maintenance and repair of equipment, and environmental services. Commitments are subject to the application of a numerical ceiling (modalities and level to be determined) except where otherwise indicated for a specific subsector, and except in Denmark, Italy, Netherlands, Sweden and the United Kingdom (with the exception of computer and related services in the United Kingdom). For independent professionals who are contractual service suppliers, access is subject to the following conditions: they must be engaged as self-employed in the supply of a service; they must have a *bona fide* contract for a period not exceeding 12 months; the entry and stay shall be for a cumulative period of not more than six months in any 12-month period or the duration of the contract, whichever is less; qualification requirements and six years of professional experience in the sector apply. Applies to: architectural services, urban planning and landscape architecture; engineering and integrated engineering services; computer and related services; management consulting services; services related to management consulting; translation services. Commitments are also subject to numerical ceilings (modalities and level to be determined) except in Denmark, Netherlands, Sweden and the United Kingdom (except for computer and related services in the United Kingdom).

- *Hong Kong, China:*[44] The previous attachment to the schedule was turned into a horizontal commitment. Applies to intra-corporate transferees who are managers, executives or specialists; detailed definitions are provided for each category. All must have been employed by their employer for at

---

44. It is unclear whether this actually represents any new offer, or simply a tidying up of the existing access set out in the attachment.

least one year prior to entry and may not change employer without approval. The commitment applies only to *bona fide* business establishments and the number of persons who may enter shall be reasonable having regard to the size and nature of the business operation. Commitments are limited to temporary stay, with appropriate authority granted prior to arrival. Stays are limited to one year in the first instance, extendable up to a total of five years.

- *Japan*: A period of one to three years specified for intra-corporate transferees, and now also includes transfers to representative offices. Specific treatment for legal, accounting or taxation service suppliers qualified under Japanese law for a period of one to three years which may be extended. A new category for natural persons who are engaged on the basis of a personal contract with a public or private organisation in Japan for activities which require technology and/or knowledge at an advanced level pertinent to physical sciences, engineering or other natural sciences; or activities which require knowledge at an advanced level pertinent to jurisprudence, economics, business management, accounting or other human sciences; or activities which require specific ways of thought or sensitivity based on experience with foreign cultures. A stay of one or three years is permitted.

- *New Zealand*: Executive and senior managers as intra-corporate transferees, specialists and/or senior personnel, and specialist personnel have, in addition to an initial period of a maximum of three years, a further period of stay up to a maximum of three years, providing the need for the worker still exists. Specialist personnel in occupations included in the Immigration Service's Occupational Shortages List are not subject to a labour market test. Service suppliers are now also permitted for the purposes of establishing a commercial presence in New Zealand.

- *Norway*: temporary entry, stay and work for managers and executives, specialists as intra-corporate transferees (provided that the service supplier is the corporation to which these are attached) is increased from a two- to four-year period. Requirement that the service must be in certain specific sectors removed.

- *Slovenia*: Removal of the reference to the "business visa" requirement for intra-corporate transferees.

- *Switzerland*: Periods of stay for essential personnel have been extended from four to five years. Experience requirements for persons employed by foreign companies for more than one year, when that company has a contract to provide services in Switzerland, have been reduced to three years from five. Additional service sectors are included for coverage: legal consultancy, auditing services, technical testing and analysis services and maintenance and repair of aircraft. Additionally, two restrictions are indicated as being under consideration for review: authorisations being subject to measures fixing the overall number of work permits; and measures limiting professional and geographical mobility within Switzerland.

Rules negotiations

In addition to the negotiations on specific commitments, there are also negotiations related to some of the main rules, or disciplines, under the GATS, which were left unfinished when the agreement was first developed in 1994. The key areas left outstanding mainly concern general disciplines and include four main areas: a possible emergency safeguard (Article X); government procurement (Article XIII); possible disciplines on trade-distorting subsidies (Article XV); and possible disciplines on certain types of domestic regulation (Article VI:4). They are explained below. These negotiations are all due to be concluded prior to the conclusion of the negotiations on specific commitments.

Emergency safeguard negotiations (Article X)

A safeguard is a mechanism that allows WTO members to temporarily suspend their commitments in the event of unforeseen and negative consequences for domestic suppliers. While such mechanisms exist for goods trade, there is currently no safeguard for services. GATS Article X mandates negotiations on the question of an emergency safeguard. Negotiations have been underway since 1996, but the original deadline has been extended several times.

Progress in the negotiations has been slow both because of differences of view among WTO members on the desirability of a safeguard, and because of technical and conceptual difficulties in developing a safeguard for services. The nature and coverage of any safeguard mechanism is still to be determined. A number of developing countries have indicated that the quality of any offers they would make would be influenced by whether or not any commitments they ultimately undertook would have access to an emergency safeguard.

Government procurement (Article XIII)

A number of important GATS provisions currently do not apply to government procurement. In particular, three key provisions do not apply: WTO members are not bound to treat all other WTO members equally (*i.e.* MFN does not apply) and commitments on market access and national treatment in a sector do not cover government procurement. Government procurement is defined in GATS as "the procurement by governmental agencies of services purchased for governmental purposes and not with a view to commercial resale or with a view to use in the supply of services for commercial sale".

GATS Article XIII mandates negotiations on government procurement in services within two years of the entry into force of the WTO Agreement (*i.e.* within two years of 1 January 1995). However, there has been relatively limited interest to date in these negotiations for a number of reasons, including the greater priority placed by a number of WTO members on concluding the safeguard negotiations and the parallel efforts to develop a multilateral agreement on transparency in government procurement which would apply to both goods and services.

Subsidies (Article XV)

There are currently no specific disciplines on subsidies under the GATS,[45] and understanding of the issue is still at an early stage. This is reflected in the language of Article XV, which states that members recognise that, in certain circumstances, subsidies may have distortive effects on trade in services. Article XV mandates members to enter into negotiations with a view to developing the necessary multilateral disciplines to avoid such trade-distortive effects of subsidies.

Article XV does not condemn subsidies *per se*, indeed, it states that the negotiations shall recognise the role of subsidies in relation to the development programmes of developing counties and take into account the needs of members, particularly developing countries, for flexibility in this area.

Article XV also mandates that members shall exchange information concerning all subsidies related to trade in services that they provide to their domestic service suppliers. In 1996, a questionnaire asked WTO members to identify any subsidies they thought were relevant. However, the survey has had relatively few responses, in part because members have experienced difficulty in identifying what might constitute a subsidy in services, particularly a subsidy with trade-distortive effects. Work on subsidies under Article XV is still at a relatively early stage.

---

45. It should be noted that discriminatory subsidies should be scheduled as a limitation on national treatment in sectors in which commitments are being made.

Box A.2. What are request and offer negotiations?

Requests

Under request-offer negotiations, each WTO member submits requests to its trading partners. These requests can be made to other members individually or to groups of members. While some countries tailor their requests to specific trading partners, others have submitted nearly identical, general requests to a number of countries.

Requests can take the form of:

o   A request for the trading partner to make commitments in a new sector (*i.e.* a sector not already included in its schedule).

o   A request to remove an existing restriction or to reduce its level of restrictiveness (*e.g.* if a country has a foreign equity limitation of 49% in a given sector, another WTO member may request that limit to be removed altogether – *i.e.* that 100% equity be allowed – or that it be raised to 75%).

o   A request to remove an existing MFN exemption.

o   A request to make an additional commitment in its schedule covering particular regulatory practices aimed at making sure that liberalisation is effective. For example, additional commitments were used in the negotiations on telecommunications for countries to commit to providing an independent regulator for the sector.

The exchange of requests has traditionally been a purely bilateral process, with countries communicating directly with one another. The WTO Secretariat does not normally play a role.

Offers

In the next stage, WTO members submit offers in response to the requests they have received. Countries usually prepare a single offer in response to all requests received. They may choose not to offer anything in response to some requests, or not to satisfy all points in some requests. The choice of what to offer is a decision of each WTO member. Some countries have already indicated that they will not be making requests or offers on particular sectors (notably, health and education) in the current round of negotiations.

For the sake of clarity, WTO members have submitted initial offers in the form of a revision to their existing schedule of commitments, with changes indicated in strike-out and bold.

While requests are addressed bilaterally to negotiating partners, offers are traditionally circulated multilaterally (*i.e.* to all WTO members). This is because, under the MFN rule, access offered to one WTO member is automatically offered to all WTO members. Given this, the offer is shown to all WTO members, and even members which did not initially make any requests can consult and negotiate with a country that has submitted an offer. Equally, some countries may choose not to submit their own requests, judging that their interests are covered by others' requests and knowing that whatever those other countries can negotiate in terms of access will automatically be extended to them under MFN (*e.g.* some countries may not use scarce administrative resources to prepare a services request of the United States if Brazil is going to request the same thing).

The submission of offers can also trigger further requests, including by countries which had not previously submitted requests. The process then continues and becomes a succession of requests and offers. As with most types of negotiations (*e.g.* pay negotiations), initial requests can be ambitious and initial offers more minimal, with a compromise emerging in the process of negotiation.

Source: Adapted from WTO Web site.

Certain types of domestic regulation (Article VI.4)

Article VI.4 mandates the development of any necessary disciplines to ensure that non-discriminatory measures relating to qualification requirements and procedures, technical standards and licensing requirements do not constitute unnecessary barriers to trade in services. That is, these measures should be:

- Based on objective and transparent criteria, such as competence and ability to supply the service.

- Not more burdensome than necessary to ensure the quality of the service.

- In the case of licensing procedures, not in themselves a restriction on the supply of a service.

These disciplines do not exist as yet. Progress on Article VI.4 has been very slow and WTO members have different views on what sort of disciplines should be developed. Some members argue that any disciplines should only focus on increasing transparency and that any "necessity test" is not necessary. Others argue that other WTO members should be free to challenge requirements they feel are trade-restrictive and be able to suggest other – equally effective and reasonably available but less burdensome – ways of achieving the same objective. Some members have also expressed concern that a necessity test could allow other WTO members to "second guess" the decisions of national regulators; others argue that a necessity test would only look at whether there were other, equally effective and reasonably available but less trade-restrictive, ways to achieve the same objective.

Annex A.1. MFN exemptions affecting movement of natural persons

A. Exemptions with comprehensive sectoral coverage

WTO members	Beneficiaries	Treatment covered	Duration	Other remarks
1. Austria	Switzerland	Waiving of visa requirement and other measures	Indefinite	
2. Brunei	Traditional sources	Preferences for entry and stay	Indefinite with periodic national review	
3. Cyprus	EU member states	Permission for limited numbers of EU nationals to be employed or to exercise professions in specific occupations in accordance with criteria to be established unilaterally or in future agreements with the EU	Until the time of full EU membership	
4. Portugal	Angola, Brazil, Cape Verde, Guinea Bissau, Mozambique, Sao Tome and Principe	Waiving of the nationality requirement for the exercise of certain activities and professions	Indefinite	
5. France	Francophone African countries, Algeria, Switzerland and Romania	Facilitation of access procedures for the exercise of certain services activities	10 years	
6. United Kingdom	Members of the British Commonwealth	Waiving of the requirement of a work permit for citizens having a grandparent born in the United Kingdom	Indefinite	
7. EC and/or member states	Switzerland	Measures with the objective of providing for the movement of all categories of natural persons supplying services	Indefinite	Reference to a progressive process
8. EC and certain member states	San Marino, Monaco, Andorra, Vatican State City	Right of establishment for natural (and legal) persons, waiving the requirement of work permits	Indefinite	
9. EC member states	States in central, eastern and south-eastern Europe including Russia, Ukraine, Belarus and Georgia, and in the Mediterranean basin	Guarantee of work permits in limited number for temporary contract work	Indefinite or, for certain countries, until an economic integration agreement is concluded or completed	All sectors (principally construction, hotel and catering). Reference to a broader initiative
10. Italy	States in central Eastern and south-eastern Europe and in the Mediterranean Basin	Guarantee of work permits for seasonal workers	Indefinite	
11. Egypt	Greece, Iraq, Jordan, Libya, Qatar, Sudan, United Arab Emirates, Yemen and possibly other countries	Full national treatment	As long as the agreements remain in force	
12. Indonesia	Malaysia, Singapore, Brunei Darussalam, Papua New Guinea, Australia	Measures concerning movement of personnel (semi-skilled workers). Limited access to low level occupations	Indefinite	
13. Jamaica	CARICOM members: Antigua and Barbuda, Barbados, Belize, Dominica, Grenada, Guyana, Montserrat, St. Kitts and Nevis, St. Lucia, St. Vincent and the Grenadines, Trinidad and Tobago	Waiving of work permits	Indefinite	
14. Liechtenstein	Switzerland	Mutual granting of temporary stay and permanent residency	Indefinite	

15. Liechtenstein	EC and EFTA countries	Preferential treatment of persons from traditional recruiting areas with regard to permits for entry, stay and work (applies to persons other than the essential persons appearing in the schedule of commitments).	Indefinite	
16. Liechtenstein	All countries	Reciprocity concerning the "right of presence of natural persons"	Indefinite	
17. Malaysia	All countries	Differential treatment for measures affecting the movement of semi-skilled and unskilled workers on a regional, religious and cultural basis	Indefinite	
18. Malta	European Union countries	Preferential treatment in the granting of licences and permits to provide services	Indefinite	Reference to the integration process into the EU
19. New Zealand	Kiribati	Most favourable entry conditions possible for up to 20 nationals each year	Indefinite	
20. New Zealand	Tuvalu	Most favourable entry conditions possible for up to 80 nationals each year	Indefinite	
21. Panama	Guatemala, El Salvador, Nicaragua, Costa Rica, and Honduras	Preferential treatment for suppliers of services of different kinds	Indefinite	
22. Panama	United States	Preferential treatment for suppliers of services under the Panama Canal Treaties	Indefinite	
23. Peru	All countries	Waiving the limitations of: three years as maximum duration, 20% of the total number of employees and 30% of the payroll	Indefinite	
24. Philippines	"All countries", countries with which a treaty on entry rights for traders and investors has been concluded	Waiving labour market test and simplifying entry procedures	Expiry or termination date of the bilateral treaties	
25. Sierra Leone	Mano River Union and ECOWAS countries	Full national treatment	As long as agreements remain in force or are extended	
26. Singapore	"Traditional sources"	Measures regarding unskilled, semi-skilled, and skilled persons except specialists and professionals. (Purpose: prevent overpopulation and maintain social order)	Indefinite (periodic national review)	
27. Solomon Islands	Members of the Melanesian Spearhead Group: Vanuatu, Papua New Guinea	Waivers for measures affecting the entry and temporary stay of natural persons	Indefinite	Reference to an ongoing process
28. Sweden	Switzerland	Measures with the objective of providing for the movement of all categories of natural persons supplying services	Indefinite	Reference to a progressive process
29. Switzerland	Liechtenstein	See 14.	Indefinite	
30. Switzerland	EC and EFTA countries	See 15.	Indefinite	

31. Tunisia	"All countries" (probably with whom Tunisia has or will have agreements)	Bilateral social security agreements: extension of social security and health benefits to citizens of other countries	Not specified	
32. Turkey	Libya	Restrictions on the transfer of premiums for long-term insurance schemes and on employment of foreign workers by foreign companies is waived (not applied *de facto*)	Indefinite	
33. Turkey	All countries	Consulate duties: if the amount of the consulate duties collected from Turkish nationals by any country is higher than the amount in the tariff list, the consulate duties collected from the nationals of that country will be increased reciprocally	Indefinite	
34. United States	All countries with which the United States has a friendship, commerce and navigation treaty, a bilateral investment treaty; or certain countries described in Section 204 of the Immigration Act of 1990	Movement of persons for trade and investment: issuance of "treaty trader or treaty investor non-immigrant visas" to nationals of the countries concerned engaged in substantial trade in services or in developing an investment	Indefinite	

B. Sector-specific exemptions

WTO member	Sector concerned	Beneficiaries	Treatment covered	Duration
1. New Zealand	Interpretation services	Japan and other countries with which such arrangements may be desirable	Most favourable entry conditions if employment for up to two years as interpreters in tourism-related industries.	Indefinite
2. Switzerland	Distribution services	EFTA members	Granting of work permits without certain limitations to employees of companies (commerce in goods) from EFTA countries	Indefinite
3. Thailand	Services mentioned in the United States-Thailand Treaty of Amity and Economic Relations	United States	National treatment to US citizens to provide the services mentioned in the Treaty	10 years
4. United States	Maritime transport	Countries that prohibit longshore work by crew members aboard US vessels	Restrictions on performance of longshore work when making US port calls by crews of foreign vessels owned or flagged in countries that similarly restrict US crews on US flag vessels.	Indefinite

Source: WTO, 1998.

Annex A.2. Negotiating guidelines

The guidelines for the negotiations[46]

GATS Article XIX requires members to establish negotiating guidelines and procedures for each round of services negotiations. These guidelines, agreed in March 2001, include the following key elements:

- Reaffirmation of some of the general principles of the GATS, including governments' right to regulate and to introduce new regulations on the supply of services in pursuit of national policy objectives and their right to specify which services they wish to open to foreign suppliers and under which conditions.

- Reaffirmation of the principle of flexibility for developing and least developed countries, as well as an undertaking that progress in the negotiations would be reviewed to check the extent to which Article IV (Increasing Participation of Developing Countries) is being implemented and to suggest ways and means of promoting the goals of that Article.

- Due consideration to be given to the needs of small and medium-sized service suppliers, particularly those of developing countries.

- No *a priori* exclusion of any service sector or mode of supply. This does not mean that all countries must make requests or offers or liberalise any particular sector, simply that no sector or mode is in principle excluded. This reflects in part the interest of developing countries in mode 4 (temporary movement of natural persons as service suppliers) and their concerns about the limited commitments that were made on this mode in the Uruguay Round, as well as the interests of a range of other countries in maritime services, where negotiations were suspended at the end of the Uruguay Round without any result, and in audiovisual services.

---

46. See "Guidelines and Procedures for the Negotiations on Trade in Services", adopted by the Special Session of the Council for Trade in Services on 28 March 2001, S/L/93, dated 29 March 2001. Available at www.wto.org.

- Establishment of the request-offer process as the main method of negotiation (see Box A.2).

- Establishment of indicative deadlines for the negotiations on rules (see above).

Article XIX also requires that, for the purposes of establishing the guidelines, the Council for Trade in Services shall carry out an assessment of trade in services in overall terms and on a sectoral basis with reference to the objectives of the agreement, including those set out in paragraph 1 of Article IV (*i.e.* which relate to increasing the participation of developing countries in world trade, including via the negotiation of specific commitments in sectors and modes of supply of export interest to them). Assessment remains a standing item on the agenda of the Council for Trade in Services.

Negotiating guidelines for least developed countries[47]

GATS Article XIX also required the development of negotiating guidelines for the special treatment of least developed countries. These guidelines were agreed on 3 September 2003 and, together with the general guidelines for the negotiations outlined above, form the basis for the negotiations and are designed to ensure the maximum flexibility for LDCs. The main points include:

- Members shall take into account the serious difficulty of LDCs in undertaking negotiated specific commitments in view of their special economic situation and shall exercise restraint in seeking commitments from LDCs.

- LDCs shall have flexibility to open fewer sectors, liberalise fewer types of transactions and progressively extend market access in line with their development situation. LDCs shall not be expected to offer full national treatment, nor are they expected to undertake additional commitments on regulatory issues which may go beyond their institutional, regulatory and administrative capacities.

- Members shall give special priority to providing effective market access in sectors and modes of supply of export interest to LDCs, and LDCs should indicate their priorities in this regard.

---

47. See "Modalities for the Special Treatment for Least Developed Country Members in the Negotiations on Trade in Services" adopted by the Special Session of the Council for Trade in Services on 3 September 2003, TN/S/13, dated 2 September 2003. Available at www.wto.org.

- Members shall take measures in accordance with their individual capacities aimed at increasing the participation of LDCs in trade in services. These could include, for example, reinforcing import/export programmes and strengthening programmes to promote investment.

- Given that LDCs have identified movement of natural persons as service suppliers under GATS mode 4 as important, members shall to the extent possible consider undertaking commitments to provide access, taking into account all categories of natural persons identified by LDCs in their request.

- The specific interests and difficulties of LDCs shall also be taken into account in the development of GATS rules.

- Targeted and co-ordinated technical assistance and capacity building programmes shall continue to be provided to LDCs to help strengthen their domestic services capacity, build institutional and human capacity and enable them to undertake appropriate regulatory reforms. Assistance shall also be provided for them to carry out national assessments of trade in services.

References

Arkell, J. (1998), "Statistics on the Presence of Natural Persons", study prepared for UNCTAD.

Chanda, R. (1999), "Movement of Natural Persons and Trade in Services: Liberalising Temporary Movement of Labour under the GATS", Indian Council for Research on International Economic Relations, India, www.icrier.res.in

Feketekuty, G. (2002), "Improving GATS Architecture" in Sherry M. Stephenson (ed.), *Services Trade in the Western Hemisphere*, Organisation of American States, Washington, DC.

Karsenty, G. (2000), "Assessing Trade in Services by Mode of Supply", in P. Sauvé and R. Stern (eds.), *GATS 2000: New Directions in Services Trade Liberalisation*, The Brookings Institution, Washington, DC.

Mattoo, A. (2003), "Introduction and Overview", in A. Mattoo and A. Carzaniga (eds.) *Moving People to Deliver Services*, World Bank and Oxford University Press, Washington, DC/Oxford.

Nielson, J. and O. Cattaneo (2003), "Current Regimes for the Temporary Movement of Services Providers: Case Studies of Australia and the United States", in A. Mattoo and A. Carzaniga (eds.), *Moving People to Deliver Services*, World Bank and Oxford University Press, Washington, DC/Oxford.

Niessen, J. (2003), "Negotiating the Liberalisation of Migration – Is GATS a Vehicle or a Model for Global Migration Governance?", paper presented at the EPC-KBF Migration Dialogue Global Governance of Migration: Challenges for the EU, Brussels 28 October, www.migpolgroup.com.

OECD (2001), "Service Providers on the Move: A Closer Look at Labour Mobility under the GATS", TD/TC/WP(2001)26/FINAL, www.oecd.org

WTO (1998), Council for Trade in Services, "Presence of Natural Persons (Mode 4): Background Note by the Secretariat", S/C/W/75, 8 December.

Young, A. (2000), "Where Next for Labor Mobility under GATS?" in P. Sauvé and R. Stern (eds.), *GATS 2000: New Directions in Services Trade Liberalisation*, The Brookings Institution, Washington, DC.

Annex B

Measuring Mode 4

This annex provides a brief sketch of what we know about the size of mode 4, both in terms of the monetary value of the trade and the number of persons moving to provide services. It uses these two parameters to demonstrate the issues that arise in trying to separate mode 4 from broader groupings of temporary foreign workers.

There are two general approaches to trying to measure trade in mode 4. First, one can try to measure the monetary value of this trade, using trade in services statistics. Second, one can try to measure the number of persons moving temporarily to supply services, drawing upon migration statistics gathered from visas and work permits. In both cases, however, there are real limits to the extent to which it is possible to obtain an accurate indication of the size of mode 4 trade.

The value of trade: statistics on trade in services

Statistics on trade in services are concerned with the monetary value of trade in services. The *Manual on Statistics for Trade in Services*[48] notes that GATS mode 4 is not well defined, nor is there a clear existing statistical framework for its measurement. The information required to measure mode 4 goes beyond what is currently or likely to be available from trade statistics (balance of payments data and foreign affiliate trade in services statistics (BPM5 and FATS) and must be supplemented, for example, by migration and labour market figures. The Manual identifies three main measures of the value of mode 4 in services: trade in services transactions, compensation of employees and workers' remittances.

Trade in services transactions between residents and non-residents includes the sales of services by movement abroad of independent service suppliers or by employees of foreign firms. These figures, which capture part

---

48. This manual was prepared by the OECD, UNCTAD, WTO, UN Statistics Division, IMF and Eurostat, with input on mode 4 from the ILO. It is available at www.oecd.org.

of mode 4 trade (sales of services by movement abroad of independent service suppliers or by employees of foreign firms), are available only for some services and allocation of trade to modes of supply is at a preliminary stage.

Compensation of employees is a very rough indicator of mode 4 trade as it includes workers in non-service sectors (manufacturing and agriculture) as well as foreign employees of local firms. Furthermore, it only covers wages, salaries and other compensation of individuals working abroad for less than one year. Although imperfect, the data on compensation of employees suggest that mode 4 trade is quite small in comparison to other modes of supply, but that it can be very important for some countries. Indeed, the figures indicate a high degree of concentration, with ten countries accounting for an overwhelming share of both imports and exports.

Workers' remittances are transfers from workers, both permanent and temporary, who stay abroad for a year or longer. They are the most commonly used proxy for mode 4 trade. However, remittances both overestimate and underestimate trade under mode 4. They overestimate by including workers other than service providers and workers who may have migrated permanently who do not fall under mode 4. They underestimate because they exclude business visitors and individuals staying less than one year abroad who do fall under mode 4. Remittances should thus be seen as only as a very rough estimate of mode 4 trade.

For many developing countries, and some developed countries (Spain, Portugal), remittances represent a substantial inflow of financial resources from abroad. Chami *et al.* (2003) estimated remittances to amount to USD 59 billion in the mid-1990s and to have steadily increased throughout the past decades (Figure B.1). The World Bank puts global remittances at USD 72 billion in 2001. (It is worth noting that remittances tend to be undercounted, as not all flows are captured in the balance of payments accounts and many remittances may not go through official channels). The World Bank (2003) also reports that, for developing countries, remittances from foreign workers are the second largest source of external funding after foreign direct investment (FDI). Between 1980 and 1999, Tunisia, Egypt and Morocco received substantially more in officially recorded remittances than in foreign aid.

In nominal terms, the top recipients of remittances included several large developing countries – India, Mexico and the Philippines – although, as share of GDP, remittances were larger in other low-income countries in 2001 (Figure B.2). Broken down along regional lines, countries in Latin America were the largest recipient of remittances in nominal terms, but relative to the size of GDP, South Asia was the largest recipient region with Sub-Saharan Africa also reporting significant shares.

Figure B.1. Worker remittances, 1970-98

Millions of USD

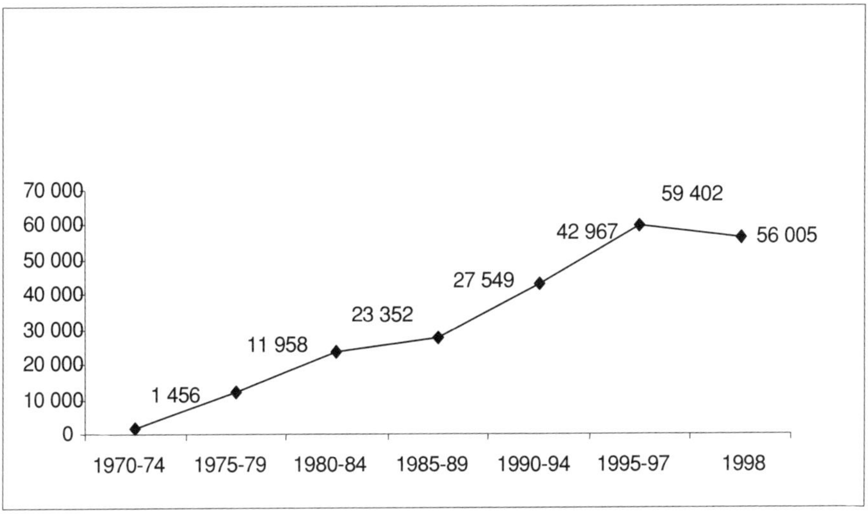

Source: World Bank as reported by Chami et al. (2003).

The number of people supplying services: migration and labour statistics

Although on an upward trend over the last decades, migration is still far below its historic peak. At its historic peak – from mid-19th century to mid-20th century – 10% of the world labour force relocated permanently across borders (World Bank, 2003). At present only 3% of the world population lives outside their country of citizenship.

Statistics on the number of people moving under mode 4 are scarce and very imprecise. While statistics are available for temporary foreign workers for a number countries, although not all, they are not an exact match to GATS mode 4. The main problems include:[49]

- Business visitors may not be separately identified and/or may enter under tourist visas. When the choice is between tourist and permanent migration visas, service providers working on "fly-in/fly-out" projects often enter as tourists. Where detailed business and tourist visa categories exist, differences in prices, conditions and the time frame for attribution of visas can create incentives for business persons to declare themselves as tourists.

---

49. For a more detailed discussion, see Nielson and Cattaneo (2003).

Figure B.2. Twenty largest recipients of remittances by ratio of receipts to GDP

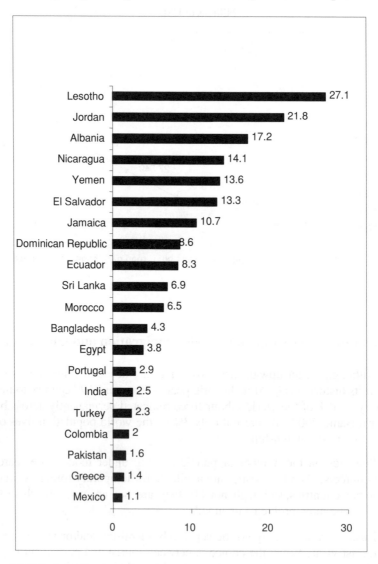

Source: World Bank (2003), adapted by authors.

- Migration statistics consider "temporary" to be 12 months or less; under the GATS, "temporary" is undefined, but in practice can be up to five years.

- Migration categories generally do not distinguish between service and non-service activities. Categories such as "managers, executives, specialists" could involve both service and non-service activities.

- It is not always possible to judge whether the activities covered by some visa categories are commercial and would qualify as the supply of a service under the GATS *e.g.* occupational trainees, sporting visas covering amateurs and professionals, and professional exchange programmes.

- Some visa categories include persons both consuming and supplying services, *e.g.* working holiday-maker schemes include persons who both consume tourism services and provide other services (*e.g.* temporary work in hospitality).

- Some national statistics include family members in the visa count of temporary foreign workers.

- "Foreign" may be defined differently for the purpose of migration statistics. Some OECD countries (*e.g.* European countries, Japan, Korea) refer to *nationality*, as citizenship laws have created a large number of people born in the country but with foreign citizenship (these people are not relevant for statistics on GATS mode 4). Countries of settlement, such as Australia, Canada and the United States, tend to use *country of birth* when producing statistics on foreign workers.

- Some movements are not recorded by visa and work permit registrations, as in the case of regional or bilateral agreements (*e.g.* within the EU, among the Nordic countries or between Australia and New Zealand). The more liberal the regime for labour mobility, the greater the difficulty in obtaining reasonably accurate statistics reflecting the extent of labour mobility.

- To gain an accurate picture of the extent of mode 4 trade, information is needed not just on the types of visa issued but on the number of actual arrivals for those visa categories. This information is often not collected or is based on sampling.

- Even where relevant visa categories exist, differences in definition mean that statistics on mode 4 entrants derived from these sources are not internationally comparable.

- While at the national level figures may be available for entries under specific visa programmes which closely correspond to mode 4 (*e.g.* temporary medical practitioner visas), no aggregate figures are available for all entrants falling under mode 4 at the national level owing to the above-mentioned problems.

- Given the absence of detailed temporary entry visa regimes in many countries, aggregate global estimates of the number of people moving to supply services under mode 4 are not possible.

So what do we know about the size of mode 4 trade?

Bearing in mind all aforementioned caveats, some initial observations can be made about mode 4 trade:[50]

- The trade represented by mode 4 service suppliers remains small compared to overall trade in goods and services and to other modes of trade in services. Nonetheless, temporary movement is very important for some industries and for some countries.

- Labour mobility of skilled workers is also increasing and seems to be concentrated in the service sectors. Movement of highly skilled workers is generally facilitated by special programmes. It is difficult to draw any conclusions about the share of highly skilled versus lower-skilled service suppliers in terms of mode 4 in overall temporary movement, as available data include workers who have entered the labour market.

- Both developed and developing countries are importers as well as exporters of temporary workers. Developed countries seem to account for the majority of both exporters and importers by some value indicators (*e.g.* compensation of employees) but not others (the major receivers of remittances are mostly developing countries). For some developing countries, labour exports are very significant compared to other forms of trade.

- While available statistics are not sufficient to draw conclusions about which countries are the primary mode 4 traders, the figures do suggest that it is not possible to draw an easy developed versus developing country picture.

- While the available statistics are poor, slightly better statistics are generally available for highly skilled workers, as these tend to be the focus of both specialised industry surveys and special work permit/migration policies.

---

50. For a more detailed discussion, see OECD (2001).

References

Chami R., C. Fullenkamp and S. Jahjah (2003), "Are Immigrant Remittance Flows a Source of Capital for Development?", IMF WP/03/189.

Nielson, J. and O. Cattaneo (2003), "Current Regimes for the Temporary Movement of Service Providers: Case Studies of Australia and the United States", in A. Mattoo and A. Carzaniga (eds.), *Moving People to Deliver Services*, World Bank/Oxford University Press, Washington, DC/Oxford.

OECD (2001), "Service Providers on the Move: A Closer Look at Labour Mobility and the GATS", TD/TC/WP(2001)26/FINAL, www.oecd.org.

World Bank (2003), "Labor Mobility and the WTO: Liberalizing Temporary Movement", Chapter 4 in *Global Economic Prospects Report*, Washington, DC.

OECD PUBLICATIONS, 2, rue André-Pascal, 75775 PARIS CEDEX 16
PRINTED IN FRANCE
(22 2004 01 1 P) ISBN 92-64-01638-4 – No. 53553 2004